ch

cherish

cherish

cherish
cherish
cherish

Reflections on the 1916 Proclamation

Hugo Hamilton • Leanne O'Sullivan

Theo Dorgan • Doireann Ní Ghríofa

Introduction by Thomas McCarthy

CORK CITY COUNCIL
COMHAIRLE CATHRACH CHORCAÍ

19
20 **16** | Clár Comórtha
Céad Bliain
Centenary
Programme

The Collins Press

First published in 2016 by
Cork City Council
City Hall, Cork, T12 T997
in association with
The Collins Press
West Link Park, Doughcloyne,
Wilton, Cork, T12 N5EF,
Ireland

Paperback ISBN: 978-1-84889-312-2

Design and typesetting by edit+ www.stuartcoughlan.com
Typeset in Baskerville

Printed in Ireland by City Print Ltd

Contents

POBLACHT NA H EIREANN.

THE PROVISIONAL GOVERNMENT
OF THE
IRISH REPUBLIC
TO THE PEOPLE OF IRELAND.

IRISHMEN AND IRISHWOMEN : In the name of God and of the dead generations from which she receives her old tradition of nationhood, Ireland, through us, summons her children to her flag and strikes for her freedom.

Having organised and trained her manhood through her secret revolutionary organisation, the Irish Republican Brotherhood, and through her open military organisations, the Irish Volunteers and the Irish Citizen Army, having patiently perfected her discipline, having resolutely waited for the right moment to reveal itself, she now seizes that moment, and, supported by her exiled children in America and by gallant allies in Europe, but relying in the first on her own strength, she strikes in full confidence of victory.

We declare the right of the people of Ireland to the ownership of Ireland, and to the unfettered control of Irish destinies, to be sovereign and indefeasible.   The long usurpation of that right by a foreign people and government has not extinguished the right, nor can it ever be extinguished except by the destruction of the Irish people. In every generation the Irish people have asserted their right to national freedom and sovereignty ; six times during the past three hundred years they have asserted it in arms. Standing on that fundamental right and again asserting it in arms in the face of the world, we hereby proclaim the Irish Republic as a Sovereign Independent State, and we pledge our lives and the lives of our comrades-in-arms to the cause of its freedom, of its welfare, and of its exaltation among the nations.

The Irish Republic is entitled to, and hereby claims, the allegiance of every Irishman and Irishwoman.   The Republic guarantees religious and civil liberty, equal rights and equal opportunities to all its citizens, and declares its resolve to pursue the happiness and prosperity of the whole nation and of all its parts, cherishing all the children of the nation equally, and oblivious of the differences carefully fostered by an alien government, which have divided a minority from the majority in the past.

Until our arms have brought the opportune moment for the establishment of a permanent National Government, representative of the whole people of Ireland and elected by the suffrages of all her men and women, the Provisional Government, hereby constituted, will administer the civil and military affairs of the Republic in trust for the people.

We place the cause of the Irish Republic under the protection of the Most High God, Whose blessing we invoke upon our arms, and we pray that no one who serves that cause will dishonour it by cowardice, inhumanity, or rapine.   In this supreme hour the Irish nation must, by its valour and discipline and by the readiness of its children to sacrifice themselves for the common good, prove itself worthy of the august destiny to which it is called.

Signed on Behalf of the Provisional Government,

THOMAS J. CLARKE.

SEAN Mac DIARMADA.   THOMAS MacDONAGH.
P. H. PEARSE.   EAMONN CEANNT,
JAMES CONNOLLY.   JOSEPH PLUNKETT.

Poblacht na hÉireann
The Provisional Government
of the
Irish Republic
To the People of Ireland

IRISHMEN AND IRISHWOMEN: In the name of God and of the dead generations from which she receives her old tradition of nationhood, Ireland, through us, summons her children to her flag and strikes for her freedom.

Having organized and trained her manhood through her secret revolutionary organization, the Irish Republican Brotherhood, and through her open military organizations, the Irish Volunteers and the Irish Citizen Army, having patiently perfected her discipline, having resolutely waited for the right moment to reveal itself, she now seizes that moment, and, supported by her exiled children in America and by gallant allies in Europe, but relying in the first on her own strength, she strikes in full confidence of victory.

We declare the right of the people of Ireland to the ownership of Ireland, and to the unfettered control of Irish destinies, to be sovereign and indefeasible. The long usurpation of that right by a foreign people and government has not extinguished the right, nor can it ever be extinguished except by the destruction of the Irish people. In every generation the Irish people have asserted their right to national freedom and sovereignty; six times during the past three hundred years they have asserted it in arms. Standing on that fundamental right and again asserting it in arms in the face of the world, we hereby proclaim the Irish Republic as a Sovereign Independent State. And we pledge our lives and the lives of our comrades-in-arms to the cause of its freedom, of its welfare, and of its exaltation among the nations.

The Irish Republic is entitled to, and hereby claims, the allegiance of every Irishman and Irish woman. The Republic guarantees religious and civil liberty, equal rights and equal opportunities of all its citizens, and declares its resolve to pursue the happiness and prosperity of the whole nation and of all its parts, cherishing all the children of the nation equally, and oblivious of the differences carefully fostered by an alien government, which have divided a minority in the past.

Until our arms have brought the opportune moment for the establishment of a permanent National Government, representative of the whole people of Ireland and elected by the suffrages of all her men and women, the Provision Government, hereby constituted, will administer the civil and military affairs of the Republic in trust for the people.

We place the cause of the Irish Republic under the protection of the Most High God, Whose blessing we invoke upon our arms, and we pray that no one who serves that cause will dishonour it by cowardice, inhumanity, or rapine. In this supreme hour the Irish nation must, by its valour and discipline and by the readiness of its children to sacrifice themselves for the common good, prove itself worthy of the august destiny to which it is called.

Signed on behalf of the Provisional Government,

THOMAS J. CLARKE

SEAN MAC DIARMADA   THOMAS MACDONAGH

P.H.PEARSE   EAMONN CEANNT

JAMES CONNOLLY   JOSEPH PLUNKETT

The wording of the Proclamation was agreed by the Military Council of the Irish Volunteers on the Tuesday before the Rising. It is generally accepted that Pearse took the lead in drafting the text, with assistance from Connolly and MacDonagh. The Proclamation was printed on Easter Sunday, on the Citizen Army's printing press, located at the rear of Liberty Hall, Dublin. Some 1,000 copies were printed.

The Democratic Programme
of the First Dáil

Members of the First Dáil, 10 April 1919
First row, left to right: Laurence Ginnell, Michael Collins, Cathal Brugha, Arthur Griffith, Éamon de Valera, Count Plunkett, Eoin MacNeill, W. T. Cosgrave and Ernest Blythe. Kevin O'Higgins is in the third row (right). Courtesy of the National Library of Ireland

We declare in the words of the Irish Republican Proclamation the right of the people of Ireland to the ownership of Ireland, and to the unfettered control of Irish destinies to be indefeasible, and in the language of our first President. Pádraig Mac Phiarais, we declare that the Nation's sovereignty extends not only to all men and women of the Nation, but to all its material possessions, the Nation's soil and all its resources, all the wealth and all the wealth-producing processes within the Nation, and with him we reaffirm that all right to private property must be subordinated to the public right and welfare.

We declare that we desire our country to be ruled in accordance with the principles of Liberty, Equality, and Justice for all, which alone can secure permanence of Government in the willing adhesion of the people.

We affirm the duty of every man and woman to give allegiance and service to the Commonwealth, and declare it is the duty of the Nation to assure that every citizen shall have opportunity to spend his or her strength and faculties in the service of the people. In return for willing service, we, in the name of the Republic, declare the right of every citizen to an adequate share of the produce of the Nation's labour.

It shall be the first duty of the Government of the Republic to make provision for the physical, mental and spiritual well-being of the children, to secure that no child shall suffer hunger or cold from lack of food, clothing, or shelter, but that all shall be provided with the means and facilities requisite for their proper education and training as Citizens of a Free and Gaelic Ireland.

The Irish Republic fully realises the necessity of abolishing the present odious, degrading and foreign Poor Law System, substituting therefor a sympathetic native scheme for the care of the Nation's aged and infirm, who shall not be regarded as a burden, but rather entitled to the Nation's gratitude and consideration. Likewise it shall be the duty of the Republic to take such measures as will safeguard the health of the people and ensure the physical as well as the moral well-being of the Nation.

It shall be our duty to promote the development of the Nation's resources, to increase the productivity of its soil, to exploit its mineral deposits, peat bogs, and fisheries, its waterways and harbours, in the interests and for the benefit of the Irish people.

It shall be the duty of the Republic to adopt all measures necessary for the recreation and invigoration of our Industries, and to ensure their being developed on the most beneficial and progressive co-operative and industrial lines. With the adoption of an extensive Irish Consular Service, trade with foreign Nations shall be revived on terms of mutual advantage and goodwill, and while undertaking the organisation of the Nation's trade, import and export, it shall be the duty of the Republic to prevent the shipment from Ireland of food and other necessaries until the wants of the Irish people are fully satisfied and the future provided for.

It shall also devolve upon the National Government to seek co-operation of the Governments of other countries in determining a standard of Social and Industrial Legislation with a view to a general and lasting improvement in the conditions under which the working classes live and labour.

Adopted by Dáil Éireann, 21 January 1919

Following the General Election held on 14 December 1918, Sinn Féin MPs refused to take their seats at Westminster, instead assembling in the Mansion House, Dublin, on 21 January 1919. They named the assembly Dáil Éireann. The drafting of the Democratic Programme was led by Thomas Johnson, leader of the Labour Party.

Reflections on the 1916 Proclamation

Cork City Council

Cork City Council believes that the Proclamation remains as relevant today as in 1916. It is important because of its content. How many documents written at the time, anywhere in the world, began with a phrase such as 'Irishmen and Irishwomen . . .'?

It is important because of the seven people who signed it, four of them were poets: Pearse, MacDonagh, Mac Diarmada, Plunkett. It was not for nothing that the 1916 Rising was called 'the poets' rebellion'.

For these reasons the *Reflections on the 1916 Proclamation* project was included in the Cork City Council Centenary Programme, launched on 7 January 2016.

The Proclamation includes inspirational phrases, such as:

> the right of the people of Ireland to the ownership of Ireland, and to the unfettered control of Irish destinies

> The Irish Republic . . . claims the allegiance of every Irishman and Irishwoman

The Republic guarantees religious and civil liberty, equal rights and equal opportunities for all its citizens

[The Republic] declares its resolve to pursue the happiness and prosperity of the whole nation and of all its parts, cherishing all the children of the nation equally.

Quite independently of the Proclamation, James Joyce's *A Portrait of the Artist as a Young Man* was published in 1916, although written over the previous decade. This novel, at least on the face of it, presents an opposing view to the sentiments expressed in the Proclamation. The text includes sentences such as:

When the soul of a man is born in this country there are nets flung at it to hold it back from flight. You talk to me of nationality, language, religion. I shall try to fly by those nets

My ancestors threw off their language and took another, Stephen said. They allowed a handful of foreigners to subject them. Do you fancy I am going to pay in my own life and person debts they made? What for?

Ireland is the old sow that eats her farrow

The Council asked four 'writers of distinction', as Thomas McCarthy puts it – Hugo Hamilton, Leanne O'Sullivan, Theo Dorgan, and Doireann Ní Ghríofa, a mix of poets and prose writers – to respond primarily to the aspirations in the Proclamation but also take into account these sentiments from *A Portrait of the Artist as a Young Man*.

James Joyce's *A Portrait of the Artist as a Young Man* was first published in 1916

Introduction

Thomas McCarthy

When Cork City Libraries and the city's Arts Office asked four writers of distinction to respond to the 1916 Proclamation they can't have imagined the brilliance and variety of the responses found here. These reports from four personal realms, of Hugo Hamilton, Leanne O'Sullivan, Theo Dorgan and Doireann Ní Ghríofa are as varied as one could ever have imagined and yet as precisely personal as one could only have dreamed. The Republic that followed the 1916 Proclamation and Rising was not a friend of the literary imagination; even writers who had proven their patriotism, Seán O'Faoláin, Frank O'Connor and Liam O'Flaherty, for example, saw their books banned and their cosmopolitanism stifled. Joyce's bitter words, forged in exile, that Ireland was the sow that eats her farrow, still seems apt and fully justified. When Sir John Keane rose in the Seanad and called the Censorship

Board a 'moral Gestapo' he was echoing the feelings of an entire generation of poets and artists. Yet our Republic has had its successes – it would be dishonest to deny the internal politics of Ireland completely. There have been good men and women who gave everything to Ireland, who carried the land safely through a World War and who had to deal with under-capitalised native industry as well as the loss of over half a million farm-labouring jobs as agriculture became mechanised. But emigration, social inequality, inadequate housing provision, and the long baleful authority of one particular Church hierarchy, all seemed beyond improvement or control. Writers like the writers here do continue to scrutinise the fruits of freedom and the persistence of social crisis in our Republic.

Reflections towards a solution continue; and creative writers are an important repository of such reflections. Here, Hamilton's intimate yet cosmopolitan day in the life of Dublin, Dorgan's characteristic, searing political analysis, O'Sullivan's backward flip into a cave of Beara habitation, Ní Ghríofa's yellow bittern-poetic gymnastics, all cohere into the widest possible contemporary response to the matter of a Republic. Hugo Hamilton brings us on a wonderful journey, so characteristic of his personal manner, so quietly stylish, where we see the conscious and unconscious inheritors of the Republic promised by our 1916 Proclamation. On an April day, one hundred years after the Rebellion, he meets a German journalist, Susanne Kippenberger, and they walk together in the rain through streets that are now inadequate for the prodigious footfall of a booming European capital city. He thinks of a self-portrait by Susanne's brother, a sad modern portrait, a work full of the sadness of dislocation, of a post-War Germany where many may never reach home; where home may never be more than a memory. Such a work of art resonates with Hamilton, it reminds him of his own nationally mixed origins. Ironically, these two rain-drenched walkers pass the windows of a German-owned shop that's displaying photographs of the 1916 leaders.

They carry on down to Moore Street where Pearse surrendered; a surrender that was decided upon in order to avoid the further slaughter of innocent civilians. While they stand under the *Dealz* archway he thinks of the meaning of this revolution in 1916, of the sense of betrayal that was felt among the thousands of Irish serving in the Somme trenches, of the madness of the quick military executions that swung public opinion and altered the course of history. Hamilton, as always, has his ear to the ground and his eye on what's contemporary – he notices the Money Transfer services, offering simple connections with Lagos, Entebbe and Manila. This is a reminder that we now share the hallowed space of Dublin and Ireland with non-nationals, with persons who have emerged from entirely different historic traumas, to share their lives with us: to make a home. 'So much has changed' he writes, 'and so has our way of gazing back at the past - it takes a hundred years to understand what happened a hundred years ago.'

In Moore Street Hamilton finds a perfect example of old and new Irish communities, all inheritors of our Republic; all working in a new spirit of live and let-live. He discovers that the old established fruit-sellers of Moore Street continue to sell their apples and oranges and yellow bananas, while the new community fruit-sellers handle only the exotic fruits – and green bananas. Thus, a very real kind of courteous non-interference is at play commercially; a communal harmony, a true Republican spirit. This happy commercial situation becomes, for Hugo Hamilton, a metaphor that contains within it the seeds of national salvation, the sense of 'home' becomes really powerful because it is a new kind of Irish home that natives and immigrants now create together. He goes on to describe the great debates about the past in Germany in the 1970s, a profound, very public encounter that became known as *Historikerstreit* – the clash of historians. He sees in this German debate lessons for Ireland, lessons on how to guide people through historical denial and come to an acceptance of the past; or, at least, a proper settlement of the past within the present, so that a country can go on and develop a truly contemporary life. Hamilton's writing here is beautiful, considered, humanist. His essay here is a treasure.

Leanne O'Sullivan creates a uniquely different encounter with the materials of the Irish past. Her world is the world of the Beara Peninsula, that place of final refuge, the stomping ground of Fenians and the impregnable fortress of Irish resistance, where the vast ocean offered the final escape route for patriots. The poet tells us how she would question her own very silent mother on the exploits of the IRB and the Easter Rising, only to be met with a wall of silence. Her mother's silence made her wonder if there was a two-fold caution at work – a fear of saying too much, but also an unspoken reverence for the great traumas of the past. There was, and is, in Beara a great respect for invisible worlds. After all it is a landscape of no less than two hundred and eighty- four circular forts, fifteen wedge tombs and twenty-four habitation caves:

> A place becomes muscular when we give it dramatic purchase, recreate it through matter and memory. In fact, it tells us more about our present selves, our imaginations, and how we think about our origins and our ends. The mythologies we build around our fears and identities endure in the landscape and weather the test of superstition.

And the poet reminds us here that 'it's a matter of minding your own business and whatever spirit is in the place will do the same.' O'Sullivan writes passionately and openly, in poetry and prose, knowing full well the effects of that mythical twilight zone of Irish being. Life in the Beara Peninsula is a mixture of topography and family story, of real landscape such as the Hag of Beara rock and silenced, unreachable habitation caves. If these caves could tell their story it would be terrible, telling us of the Tudor clearances through burning, murder and exile, a narrative captured by the colonist Edmund Spenser in his *Special View of Ireland*, a view that so reeks of anti-Irish racism that it cannot be treated with a grain of respect; yet it contributed to a key colonial attitude to the 'mere' Irish. It was attitudes such as Spenser's and competing truths known by the makers of Beara myth that set alight a deadly fight for possession of land and facts, a fight for definition that would end in flames in 1916. A poet like O'Sullivan, a female poet and thus placed outside history, as Eavan Boland has written, can only leap backwards into the dark cave of the Irish past; and this has been Leanne O'Sullivan's method in dealing with the atavistic materials of our Irish history. 'Fair? Don't talk to me about fair./ When I came to the river in spate/I could only carry one of my two/ companions across it with me' she writes in 'The Cailleach to the Widow.' In writing like this she has combined both a re-possessive instinct for myth-making and a humane, social consciousness. The truth of the Proclamation for her lies somewhere in that space created by a silent mother and a mother's myth-creating daughter. The past lies beneath everything, to be discovered like this:

> A penny dropped
> a hundred years ago
> turns up beneath
> our sweetheart cabbage
>
> ('Heirloom')

Those who have followed the work of Theo Dorgan over the past decades, this poet of voyages and praxis, this poet of public service and high aestheticism, will know what to expect in terms of commitment and definition when it comes to the matter of Ireland. His Ireland is a clearly and completely defined republic, a place worthy of James Connolly. He begins his own response by tackling the contests of definition that have plagued Republican life in Ireland:

As is all too common in Irish politics, there are absurdities at work here: the actually-existing but formally unclaimed Republic is at odds with the theological Republic-to-be-established. We have a Republic that decries 'Republicans', and 'Republicans' who disdain and grant only a partial legitimacy to the Republic most of us think we live in.

Dorgan goes on to outline the sad neglect, the public avoidance of any definitions of the Republic, by the intellectual and administrative elites in Ireland. When he published a major collection of essays on a possible future Republic-defining constitution he was met with a wall of silence; only SIPTU's paper reviewed the work. He surmises, correctly, that the powers-that-be in our Republic avoid the embarrassment of such defining efforts. He goes on to recall that the Democratic Programme of the First Dáil had been drawn up by Thomas Johnson and William O'Brien, with the participation of Cathal O'Shannon. Ironically, it was that great advocate of later massive Public Housing programmes, Seán T. O'Kelly who toned down the more socialist elements in this Programme. The radicalism implicit in the words of the 1916 Proclamation could not survive the proprietorial nationalist cadres who have always been the bulwark of Irish separatism. Any tendancy towards Bolshevism within the Irish political family in 1916-1923 needed to be eradicated, or at least rendered neutral.

Dorgan, first and foremost a Socialist poet since early youth, tries to bridge that gap between 1916 radicalism and the comfortable bourgeois laissez-faire of current Irish politics. He has always tried to bridge this gap by an honest effort of theorising; theory and policy expression being the only options open to a democratic socialist operating upon the *res publica*, the matters public. Dorgan has worked tirelessly to add value and depth to our political discourse; his brilliant effort here is yet another example of heavy lifting on behalf of the nation. "In our stalled republic," he writes, "the political class has continued in the habit of pretending they mean certain things while we, the electorate, happily pretend to believe them. This corrosive ambiguity, on both sides, from the very start laid the foundations for the emergence of a disdainful state-management class of professional politicians and senior civil servants, and at the same time for mass defection from political responsibility on the part of a citizenry reduced to a rubber stamp electorate." All of which defies the programme implicit in the words of the Proclamation, "to pursue the happinness and prosperity of the whole nation and of all its parts, cherishing all the children of the nation equally." Dorgan's historical sweep, his understanding of 1916 combined with his ability to detect the cumulative effect of national hypocracy, makes of his essay an important witness document. It is a work worth studying.

The rhymed and half-rhymed couplets of Doireann Ní Ghríofa call us back into an intensely personal response to what was proclaimed in 1916: "Its capitals call still, to **IRISHMEN AND IRISHWOMEN/** in mismatched fonts, just as it did in its beginning." The frail paper upon which the words of Connolly and Pearse are printed become, for the poet Ní Ghríofa, a metaphor of all humble origins. Humble origins when they cohere become a powerful new force; this is one of the first messages contained in her lyrical response. In 'For our Sisters, Another Proclamation' Ní Ghríofa freeze-dries the Proclamation, sparing only the inky parts that cohere into a gender-relevant witness document; what is essential survives in her post-modern text. The code words contained in Witness Statement 94 of the Bureau of Military History, the statement of young Mary McLoughlin, that strange 'Béalrún,' was the final instruction she received from Thomas MacDonagh:

> It was only four syllables – Yellow Bittern –
> the title of a poem he had translated
>
> based on the poem An Bonnán Buí. These, the
> last words chosen by Mac Donagh to send to
> his friend
> as their battle drew to its end: a bird that died
> of thirst,
> its body left stretched on a frozen lake.

Her work here is a marvelous response to the meaning of MacDonagh's encoded message. Her linguistic playfulness (she is an expert poet in both Irish and English) combined with an instinctive feminism creates a unique document here – the statement that can be read online* – becomes a living element within what is an historical essay as contemporary installation. Hers is a fabulous response made uniquely useful by the intervention of a woman's voice from that day of Irish surrender and definition. What is personal seems vulnerable when placed against the juggernaut of history and peer-reviewed historical commentary, but Ní Ghríofa sees history not as a sounding board for the declared republic but as a sounding-board for the heart of Mary McLoughlin. The work in its entirety becomes the most intense artistic response possible. It is a triumph of the human over the historical; it believes in anecdote rather than theory. In the end what is good for a Republic is not a metaphysical question, but a personal one.

These essays with their four distinct yet fully-developed personal voices are a tribute not just to a theory of our Republic, but to the endurance of the human spirit. They are four blessings upon the heart of our enduring nation.

THOMAS McCARTHY
September, 2016

*www.bureauofmilitaryhistory.ie/reels/bmh/BMH.WS0934.pdf#page=3

RISH

...tered control of Irish destinies, to
...on of that right by a foreign peopl

Proclamations

Hugo Hamilton

It's April 2016 – a Tuesday afternoon, raining heavily. I make my way along O'Connell Street, the spire is pointing into the clouds, a motionless tricolour over the GPO, seagulls hunched up on the roof. I am on my way to the Gresham Hotel to meet a journalist from Berlin. She has come to Dublin to write about the 1916 commemorations. She wants to hear what the proclamation means to us now and how Ireland has changed in the past hundred years since the Easter Rising.

She stands in the reception area of the Gresham Hotel with a small umbrella by her feet. She smiles and says the rain reflects all German expectations of Ireland. Her name is Susanne Kippenberger. Her brother was the famous German artist Martin Kippenberger who belonged to a wave of radical art in post-war Germany. She wrote a wonderful biography of his strange and erratic life. There is a great self-portrait of him with a sign around his neck saying '*Bitte Nicht nach Hause schicken*' (Do not send home please).

In that painting he bears a sad expression, like a lost child, a man who cannot find his way and has nowhere to go. It seems to say everything about the world we live in. Or maybe I read into it so much of myself and my own dislocated relationship with home and identity and where I belong. Perhaps we're all a bit lost now, that's what I have come to think. Perhaps we have discovered that home is no longer some fixed location but something that has gone missing inside us. Home is a memory. We like to remember where we come from but we don't want to be sent back to the past.

Susanne is keen to get out into the streets in spite of the rain. She has already been to visit the GPO exhibition, so I suggest Moore Street where the Easter rebellion came to an end in 1916. We cross O'Connell Street and make our way into Parnell Street. Her umbrella is inadequate. The pavements of Dublin are inadequate. The volume of foot traffic is too heavy for the spaces designed a hundred years ago. We fight our way into a stream of oncoming pedestrians rushing through the rain. Now and again two umbrellas clash and spin, like colliding planets, sending a shower of drops in all directions, the faces underneath smiling apologetically. We come around into Moore Street. I want to show Susanne the spot where Patrick Pearse surrendered to the British forces and handed over his sword in a great symbolic gesture as though he was on stage and the world was his audience.

At the top end of Moore Street there is an outlet belonging to the German supermarket chain Lidl. They have got into the spirit of 1916. They have erected photographs of the Irish revolutionaries above the entrance of the store to mark the centenary commemorations.

We carry on down Moore Street to the place where the revolution-aries spent the last hours of the rebellion, where they had tunnelled from one building to the next and considered their hopeless position. It must have crossed their minds in that dismal ending that their vision of Ireland may have been seen by so many Irish people as a profound failure, they were regarded as plain thugs, the word rebel had not yet acquired that glorious ring.

We take shelter under an archway and stand looking at a broad green canvas across the upper windows of the memorial buildings bearing the words with which the rebel leaders announced their surrender –

> in order to prevent further slaughter of Dublin citizens, and in order to save the lives of our followers, now surrounded and hopelessly outnumbered...

We talk. We go over Irish history. The executions turned the leaders of the rebellion into martyrs. The brutal finality of this episode gave Irish people a reason to be proud and aggrieved – it led to the formation of an independent Irish state.

To the British in command, the leaders of the 1916 rebellion were committing an act of treason. The signatories of the proclamation had mentioned 'our gallant allies in Europe', meaning the Germans, the very enemy the British were facing in the trenches. It is believed that the calculated inclusion of Britain's greatest enemy compelled the British forces to execute these men like common deserters on the battlefield. Their bodies were buried in an unmarked plot to prevent any shrine to their memory.

So we're standing under the archway next to DEALZ store, talking about the 1916 proclamation. Behind us, the mobile phone shops and internet call centres. There are signs offering money transfer services, cheap flights to Lagos, Entebbe, Manila. It becomes clear how much time has gone by since the leaders of the rebellion gave up their fight here in April 1916. So much has changed and so has our way of gazing back at the past – it takes a hundred years to understand what happened a hundred years ago.

Along the street are the stalls selling fruit. These famous Moore Street vendors had to fight to retain their right to keep these stalls not so long ago. Dublin city authorities wanted to remove them from the street but they held on. The stalls now consist of uniform steel trolleys on wheels, covered by canopies of blue and white striped canvas.

I remember passing by these vendors on my way home from school in Parnell Square. They used to sell their fruit from carts, from converted prams, from improvised wooden trolleys. They sold apples and oranges and bananas and sometimes from year to year they added a new fruit, like kiwis or mangoes. They sold vegetables – cauliflower and cabbages, carrots and potatoes. You heard the chant along the street, announcing the price for a dozen oranges. At Halloween, they sold peanuts and pumpkins. You could buy fireworks, imported illegally from Northern Ireland, which the women pulled out from under their dresses – *do you want bangers, love?*

The vendors still carry the same range of fruit and vegetables they sold fifty years ago. A pyramid of oranges with a cardboard sign stuck at the top – 8 for 2 euros. Apples

– 6 for 2 euro. Tomatoes in an open box set at an angle, pears wrapped individually in paper. Over the years they have added green peppers and red peppers, red onions, garlic. We hear two women under the arch calling out – tobacco, cigarettes. They call the words out like fireworks. They look a bit anxious seeing Susanna making notes.

Moore Street has, over the years, become a great mixture of traditional Dublin vendors and a whole new set of traders from all over the world. Like the African hair extension shops, the Asian markets, the Transylvanian shop which carries a wide variety of Polish and Romanian goods, cured meats that were not here fifty or a hundred years ago. They have a sign saying – the taste of Romania. Underneath, another notice warning customers that goods cannot be returned if the packet has been opened, so you cannot help thinking that people sometimes buy produce like ham or salami which then turns out not to taste anything close to what they were expecting, they feel misled.

At one end of the street you have Anne's Hot Bread shop, selling all the traditional Irish fare like chocolate doughnuts and cream doughnuts with the squiggle of red jam – the jam lights up like the glow of a heating bar across the white cream. Their hot food includes chicken in cream sauce, beef stew and roast potatoes, and chips. A hundred metres down the street there is an Asian restaurant selling none of these things, their menu offers all kinds of Chinese and Thai street food including Chicken Teriyaki – pay before you eat.

Along the street you hear the languages of the world. You see women in long, colourful African dresses, women with headscarves, children with hair tied in tiny black curls, and passing by through all that mixture of nationalities, a group of history tourists being led through the street on a tour of 1916 hotspots. They stop to take pictures of the memorial buildings where the rebellion ended.

Behind us, under the arch, there are a number of shops selling exotic fruit and vegetables that are not available at the traditional stalls along the street. At one of the new stalls we see white courgettes, green courgettes, okra, small aubergines, red and green chilis, very hot peppers, shallots, whole and quartered watermelon. Underneath, there are boxes with several varieties of root crops like sweet potatoes, yams, lotus root, eddoes that look like brown hairy potatoes.

They sell a lumpy green fruit like a courgette with warts. It turns out to be white kerelia – with an explanation underneath for those like me who have never seen this fruit before – White bitter melon – 10 euros a kilo. And another more scary item, round and spiky, twice the size of a football and looking more like it came from the deep sea and could still be alive. It turns out to be a sweet jackfruit from India – 250 euros.

They don't sell ordinary potatoes, I remark to Susanne. They don't sell apples and oranges. They sell small green bananas from Kenya but they do not sell normal yellow bananas. They sell sticks of raw sugar cane, but they don't sell pineapples.

The sky was clearing up. It stopped raining. There was a lot more to be said about the Proclamation, about Ireland and about the distance we have travelled in a hundred years, but we take the opportunity to step out and look at the fruits stalls on the street. There seems to be a strict line of demarcation in trade. The list of fruit and vegetables sold by traditional vendors seems to remain diligently separate, there is no cross-over, they don't sell okra or aubergines.

At one of the street stalls I ask the woman where the bananas are from.

Ireland, she says.

Come on. Bananas don't grow in Ireland.

Everything good comes from Ireland, she says.

We laugh. I recognize that Irish way of avoiding the question. Here it is – what my German mother could never come to terms with, that imaginative Irish way of side-stepping. All her life, my mother continued to expect people to speak straight. It's worth admiring the Irish talent for detours, that devious way with language may have led us down the path to literature and song instead of mathematics and military precision. We don't do war very well, we do proclamations, insurrection, but we don't have that meticulous intuition needed to conquer other nations.

The 1916 Rising was never going to be a military success. It was a poetic success, a triumph of the imagination. It became a piece of theatre, a rebellion of poets and thinkers. There would have been far more practical ways of fighting a war, such as the guerrilla war of independence that came later. The Easter Rising was a piece of street drama, what you would now call a site-specific stage play, with consequences.

For decades now, there has been a heated debate going among intellectuals in Ireland over the justification of the

1916 rebellion. Did the rebels have entitlement to rebellion? I try to position the debate in a European context. In Germany in the 1980's, a notorious argument developed among historians over the interpretation of history and the crimes of the Nazi years. It was called *Historikerstreit* – the clash of historians. It became a defining moment in German thinking whereby the idea of minimizing or 'relativizing' Nazi crimes by comparing them to world horrors such as slavery and other colonial crimes, for example, became untenable. It was at this point that German people began to recognize that Nazi crimes had no equal, there was no way of pointing the finger anywhere but at the themselves. This is what led to the unique way in which the Germans carefully went about dealing with their history. It was this painstaking and unequivocal way of examining the past over generations which has brought Germany to a place of profound understanding. That acknowledgement of Nazi crimes has become Germany's greatest achievement.

We have been trying to face our history in Ireland with a similar kind of honesty. We have, for example, made the connection between the Easter Rebellion and the physical force tradition which later led to a bombing campaign in which so many people died over the course of the Troubles. I remember the shock of seeing the interiors ripped out of pubs in Birmingham. I remember the white dust covered faces of the injured. I remember the faces of the six innocent men who were wrongfully convicted for the crime.

The past offers so much opportunity to feel hurt. It's easy to write history backwards and equate the word rebel with terrorist. It was easy to put the crimes of the provisional

IRA down to a cause that originated with the leaders of the 1916 Rising. Because Patrick Pearse and James Connolly had initiated an armed conflict, taking over buildings in Dublin by illegal force, historians were able to recast the rebellion as the precursor to all politically motivated violence ever since.

It is, I suggest to Susanne, our clash of historians.

Since the 1970's, Irish history was placed in the context of the raging troubles in Northern Ireland. The 1916 leaders were accused of having no mandate from the Irish people to carry out a rebellion against the Crown. It was undemocratic to fight for independence. The argument has become difficult to sustain in this year of commemoration – what revolution gathers a petition to prove its mandate from the people before it strikes out on the path to freedom?

It was only after the executions that the people of Ireland gave their majority support to the act of rebellion. So the argument still remains – if you acknowledge the right to unlawful rebellion in 1916, then you automatically acknowledge the right of any wrongheaded minority to carry out further unlawful armed actions awaiting future approval from the people. We feel so grown up when we look back. But can we force history to behave like the present?

Not for one minute can I imagine Patrick Pearse leaving a bomb in a pub full of innocent people. Not for one minute can I imagine James Connolly carrying out the killing of Jean McConville, the mother of ten children, accused of being an informer, taken from her family in Belfast and shot in the back of the head, then buried in an unmarked location which her killers refused to reveal to the family for decades. There is nothing in the proclamation which sanctions the atrocities that came after, nothing justifying unconditional violence, nothing about the basic codes of humanity that has changed in a hundred years.

Is it even worth getting into that clash of historians?

Is it not better to see the Irish proclamation for the generous, vision-ary and inclusive instinct set out in the words of the signatories? We look back from a place of safety. The Proclamation can now be read by Irish people right around the world on the anniversary of the Rising, knowing that it has brought us democracy. It has given us the right to trade our democracy with other democracies.

At another stall on Moore Street, possibly the very spot where Patrick Pearse surrendered a hundred years ago, I ask the vendor the same question – where are your bananas from?

Bananaland, she says.

She calls me sweetheart and smiles. When I pursue it, she points at the tag on the bananas, reads it out like we're in geography class together – Colombia.

Colombia. Where is that?

Far away, love.

I follow my curiosity and ask her straight out why she doesn't sell any of the exotic fruit sold in the Asian shops. In a capitalist economy, every commercial opportunity is worth exploring at least. If there are customers around who buy fruit with warts and spikes, then why doesn't she take the chance and sell them, it's a free market.

> They sell to their own people, the woman says.
> They have their own ways and their own things
> they want to eat.

So there is an unspoken deal between them, a courtesy agreement to limit sales along cultural lines? Maybe the Moore Street vendors don't feel genuine selling sweet potatoes, they keep their monopoly on traditional fruit from far away while the Asian vendors have a free run at the exotic fruit from far away. The only thing in common, it seems, is root ginger. Root ginger is free to travel across the cultural frontiers on Moore Street. And for some reason the traditional traders sell passion fruit, perhaps they belong to the same family of apples and oranges?

At one of the Asian shops I ask the same question, why they don't sell apples and oranges. I quickly get the obvious explanation that they don't want conflict with the traditional vendors.

> We work together with the local merchants,
> an Asian man at the till says to me. We don't
> compete, we compensate.

They work in harmony. The traditional Irish and the new Irish, working together, still separated along taste and cuisine, still clinging to their own list of fruit and vegetables, living a perfect coexistence.

Patrick Pearse would be proud.

The Proclamation may even have anticipated this coexistence of cultures. It has made provisions for including all people living in Ireland. It aspires to the ideals of cherishing the children of the nation equally. The famous words undersigned by the leaders of the rebellion have brought on another flourishing debate this year which looks at the homeless, the people who have no work, the people with no future in a capitalist society, those who are disenfranchised and remain outside the aspirations set out in the Proclamation. The words of the Proclamation return us to that open challenge – have the people of Ireland achieved the goals on which the liberation of their country was founded.

The Proclamation has, for example, brought us to a place where we held a referendum on same sex marriage. It's taken a hundred years, but we live in a nation free to make the decision which now sees gay people as legal and equal, no longer forced into internal hiding.

So much is being said of the revolution this year and how the memory of 1916 excluded women. The famous photograph taken of Patrick Pearse surrendering on Moore Street always appeared as though he was alone. Nurse Farrell who stood beside him was removed from memory. It was not the people who took part in the rebellion who removed women from this moment in history. It was the Catholic State which emerged after independence which found the hero status of women too difficult to deal with. Unlike Rosa Luxemburg and other female heroes of resistance elsewhere, Irish Catholic thinking found female revolutionaries too toxic, too difficult to control as a narrative, too much competition for the Virgin Mary, so they were firmly struck out.

I recall teaching students at the University in Bucharest just after the fall of Communism, discussing with them how the British regime in Ireland was so easily replaced by a new regime of Catholic hierarchy – the horse remains the same, the horseman is exchanged. They argued with my harsh view of Catholicism. In their eyes, religious belief was a form of oppositional force, it became a way of expressing resistance to the Communist dictatorship of Ceauçescu. They were right, of course. It was that way in Ireland too. We remember the Mass rocks and the persecution of priests. It was religion, more than any other belief in political freedom which provided opposition to the British regime Ireland. In Romania, Ceauçescu took over monasteries and expelled religious orders from their churches, took them over for his own private use. It brought home to me why the Catholic Church acquired such a hero status in the new independent Irish state, why priests had such cool – I equate the old word holy with the current word cool – why it became such a blessing in Ireland to have a priest in the family, why the country went into a spin of holiness.

In 1959, the German writer Heinrich Böll lovingly described the rainfall in Achill Island. In his classic collection of travel essays on Ireland, he also observed the rising anxiety at the time over Nelson's Pillar. In the new republic, the idea was being put forward to replace Admiral Nelson, still towering over the city since the days of the British Empire, with a figure that would reflect the modern Irish independent state – the Virgin Mary.

I am one of those Irish people who can remember Nelson's Pillar before it was blown up fifty years ago. One afternoon, against my father's will, my brother and I were taken up the winding staircase inside the pillar by an aunt. We stood inside the cage at the top and looked out across the city. We didn't say much. We loved her for bringing us to a place that was forbidden. We didn't stay long, just long enough to see Dublin from a point of view that had already gone out of existence. And then I remember standing one morning on my way to school, looking at the stump of the pillar like something amputated. The street looked unfamiliar. The past was missing. The rubble of the empire, you might call it, was everywhere and the windows in the shops nearby were smashed. They were singing songs about the admiral. His head went off to Australia, as I remember. It was clear to me that I had been present in a place that was now moving swiftly behind us into the deep past.

The commemorations fifty years ago now look so much like an unfinished war in which we were still afraid of the monuments left behind by the British. It felt like some kind of political superstition, Nelson still operating his voodoo control over the people until he was removed, like all those enormous statues of Stalin were removed after the fall of Communism, like we are now in the process of removing, or making harmless, the strict icons of Catholicism. There was a triumphant atmosphere in Ireland fifty years ago, the country was full of anger, so eager to get even, so full of corporal punishment and abuse, so much in need of putting the past right that we could only inflict the injustice on ourselves. Was there some kind of post-colonial self-loathing that we all passed around inside the families? In the sixties we had the sounds of freedom coming towards us from abroad, but we were still locked in a struggle with self-pride. We were still blaming Britain for everything. We had the aftertaste of empire, maybe it was a kind of buried nostalgia, we admired our greatest enemy like a lost friend – we found the absence hard, we had yet to take responsibility for our own mistakes.

The buses in 1966 all had crossed swords on the engine grills. There was a torch of freedom on every lamppost. No wonder it was followed soon by the troubles in the North. At school in Colaiste Mhuire in Parnell Square, we took part in a pageant that went over every painful moment in our history, like a series of lost hurling games. I got the part of a croppy boy in a white shirt and a green sash around the waist, holding a pike from 1798, I had to die on stage every night.

The commemorations this year have become so generous by comparison. They reflect the huge confidence which the Irish have acquired in the past fifty years. We have now restored the women of 1916. We have come around to saying that Nurse Farrell had her feet erased from the famous photograph beside Patrick Pearse surrendering. We have come around to acknowledging that she was buried alongside her female lover and partner. The revolution was not merely a political one, it became a much wider rebellion which eventually had to be fought over our way of dealing with memory.

That is the nature of revolution, it's never over. The daily revolution, my father called it, by which he meant the restor-ation of the Irish language as the principle language of the Irish people, with the English language relegated. His vision of revolution was narrowed to that single cultural battleground. He was born in 1913, he was among the first generation in charge of the new independent nation after 1921, his view was one of cultural liberation which involved using our heritage as a weapon of de-colonization. As I put it in my memoir *The Speckled People*, we were conscripted into a language war, we stood as children at the seafront throwing stones at the waves, holding back British culture from our shores.

Each generation has to liberate itself from the generation before it. Our fathers turned to the Catholic church and to the Irish cultural revival. The next generation turned back to Britain, to a new wave of rock and roll coming across to rescue us from Catholicism. Our deep historical connection to Britain gave us an early taste of the global world, it gave us a global language and a global view.

The daily revolution, from our point of view, involved a more essential battle with the blindness of faith. It was the freedom of women to be treated as equal which became more pressing, a kind of breakthrough which ultimately liberated men from their dominant patriarchal role as much as it liberated women from their subservient role. It is not hard to look back at the way things were in Ireland once and to think this kind of freedom will come to other places in the world still struggling with the same issues of dominance over women. We now know the expanding aspirations of the revolution. The equality referendum last year seems like the high point of the 1916 Rebellion and its long aftermath. If there was a deficit in democracy it was certainly put right at this moment in our history. It takes time, but the freedom we ask for comes by small degrees.

Susanne and I stand on Moore Street, we compare the Kenyan green banana with the Colombian yellow banana. At one of the shops I buy a packet of plantain chips. Now there's something new – plantain crisps. I get the feeling Ireland can get used to anything new, take on every taste, it's all part of our way of looking outwards.

Our place among nations.

I put it to Susanne that there were two proclamations made in 1916 – one signed by seven revolutionaries declaring an independent nation for Ireland and read out on Easter Monday outside the GPO by Patrick Pearse – the other took the form of literature, a kind of memoir/novel written by James Joyce called *The Portrait of the Artist as a Young Man* in which the narrator Stephen Dedalus turns his back on the political solution by force of arms and declares freedom or artistic expression as the essential principle of liberation.

The Joyce proclamation took time getting through to us because we were still so caught up in the idea of national freedom and the rigid expression of our Irish identity. Joyce was banned, he didn't get a mention in school, he was not allowed into the house, he was regarded as dirty, un-Catholic.

It was only later that we understood how instead of becoming a signatory to the GPO Proclamation he coined his own aesthetic way of liberating the intellect from the 'nets' that threatened to trap him in his own country. It was Patrick Pearse who taught Joyce Irish. Joyce was fully aware of the aims of the political enterprise of freedom from British rule, but he turned to his own literary revolution.

In the *Portrait* Joyce speaks of his refusal to join the physical force tradition. The only arms he will bear are those of 'silence, exile and cunning.' The same weapons we Irish people were using against each other all the time, you might say, only that Joyce took them away to Trieste and gave it all back to us in the form of great art.

It's June 2016 – the Easter Rising Commemorations have passed by now. At Kilmainham Jail in late April, a site-specific event called *Signatories* was performed consisting of a series of monologues by Irish writers in response to the executions and directed by Patrick Mason. I wrote the part of a young woman looking back at James Connolly from the present day. At the end of the piece she sings a song written by John Lennon – he always felt close to the visionary thinking of Connolly – a working class hero.

A working class hero is something to be…

On a more grand scale, RTÉ designed a commemorative event which was performed and televised from the Bord Gáis Theatre in Dublin. It was epic and glorious – on an operatic level – no lonely sean-nós singers unaccompanied, no echoing lament on the tin whistle, no ballads about the heather blazing. It reflected all the self-confidence we have become used to as Irish people in recent times. It made Irish people feel good about themselves. The public reaction was full of a new kind of emotion, perhaps the emotions we feel now are more designed by healing and self-care and winning attitudes. Our collective national moments are full of success and knowing that we are admired around the world, even envied. We are proud of ourselves. We respect ourselves. Being Irish is a great achievement. Who in their right minds would not want to be Irish today? We have placed ourselves on the world stage in so many cultural and creative ways. People come to live here and see the brightness of our cities in the way that we saw the brightness of foreign cities to which we escaped. The newcomers see the arches under the bridges lit up green, the up-lights in the streets illuminating the ghostly trees from underneath. We have a national image which has emerged out of painful times and is now full of luck and optimism, an image that makes us feel right about the past, a history that makes us special, unique, different, like no other country on earth.

All this confidence allowed the Bord Gáis Theatre performance to become a shiny event, it showed strength and power, it was expensive. The grief over the past has become uplifting. The hurt is positive. We celebrate our failures. There were no croppies dying, no blood soaked shirts. It was all about courage – our creativity, our ambitions, our targets. The 1916 executions were portrayed in a solemn dance movement in which dark, faceless human figures slowly dropped to the floor. The show included a singer rendering the powerful words of Patrick Pearse about his vision of great beauty – *Fornocht a chonac thú* – naked I saw you – the same naked beauty which Yeats described so famously as a terrible beauty. We live right inside that terrible beauty now and we love it.

Ireland is an old country. The landscape is full of memory. The past is spread out in every direction, it's there in the signs, the old ghost language continues shadowing every place name. The Aer Lingus flight attendant still speaks that ghost language welcoming people to Dublin when they land. This is an ancient place, but it continues to feel like a young country just growing up, like we have just achieved our freedom and we have come out from under all that self-repression of the past. The ghost language is still following us around.

Around the country over Easter, scenes of the revolution were re-enacted to allow the moment of liberation to be felt in a real way on the ground. It seems like we sometimes strain to believe our own history. Something about the nature of re-enactment that undermines our ability to process what happened in the past without having to see it performed live in front of us. I went on the Dublin Bus 1916 tour and found it all a bit frightening, being trapped on the upper deck with black out curtains and actors staging the rising, shouting at the passengers. At one point, one of the actors, in costume from 1916, sat with her knees up in front of me, maybe a bit like Molly Bloom, or Molly Malone, maybe a mixture of both, I couldn't make out who she wanted to be, but she stared at me and asked me who I was. I didn't want to admit that I was there on this 1916 tour, so I said I was Joseph Plunket and she laughed. The actors gave their performance, there was smoke around the upper deck, it was hard to breathe. A soldier, meant to be one of the Irish rebels but dressed in First World War British uniform, maybe that was easier to hire, came running upstairs with a Lee-Enfield rifle, aiming out the windows over the heads of the passengers. He then died in the arms of the woman who looked like Molly Malone and she said – don't leave me, don't die.

I don't know what I was doing getting on that bus in first place. I have an irrational fear of re-enactments. It may come from the time when I had to die repeatedly as a croppy boy in our school pageant. I should relax and say to myself that as long as we do re-enactments of war, it's a good sign, it means we are not really at war, we are not in the business of killing, just playing war. But I still don't trust re-enactment as a way of understanding anything or preventing anything from happening again. I had the same response to seeing playing soldiers in Gettysburg in order to bring the American civil war back to life. Are the glorious moments more suited to re-enactment, I wonder? Will it be possible to stage the less glorious highlights of the Irish civil war? Perhaps I see this kind of thing simultaneously from the German side of myself and think of so many historical moments that would be impossible to re-enact.

Or maybe I'm wrong, maybe one of these days they will get around to presenting re-enacted versions of the most grotesque moments of European history, perhaps simulating in virtual reality what is beyond understanding on the scale of crimes against humanity. You will be able to put on glasses and go deep inside those times of horror like you don't believe anything in history is true until you see it with your own eyes.

It's June 2016 – I'm in Trieste at the invitation of the Trieste Joyce School. And maybe it is this warm city on the Mediterranean to which Joyce fled from Ireland that opens up so many explanations about our own country. It's easy to see why the city offered Joyce such great freedom as an artist. He was out of Dublin, free to write about his mother city, no longer bound by the nets of Catholicism and nationalism. Trieste is a sunny place along the coast, not unlike Dublin in some ways, but when Joyce arrived, the city was at a peak of its great cosmopolitan past.

When Joyce came here, leaving his wife Nora on a bench while he got involved in a sailor's brawl and came back to find her still sitting there hours later, the city had a multiple-ethnic population. Walking the streets he must have marvelled at the diversity of nationalities. There were seven different religions, the city was full of people from Slovenia, from Croatia, from Austria, there was a huge community of Jews living there at the time. And maybe this is what unleashed his greatest literary enterprise, the creation of the figure of Leopold Bloom, the person who is native but is never accepted as belonging to his own country.

Bloom is a man cheated, wandering like a newcomer around his own city, the man who is being asked – *what is your nation?*

Ulysses became the literary discovery of the twentieth century, not merely for the internal dialogue and the sheer artistic invention in the prose, but for this elevation to the centre stage of the outsider among us. Joyce is more than a modernist genius, he is far more contemporary, his writing is for now, for the migrant, for all the people who are not quite accepted. He shows us the shame and the dignity of the stranger.

Trieste is built on the grand model of Austro-Hungarian cities like Vienna and Graz and Budapest. It is easy to compare the Habsburg Empire with the European Union, it may have been a forerunner of the EU before the it fell asunder in the First World War. When Joyce returned to Trieste after that war the city had already changed, the ethnic tensions had begun to dissolve that great moment of co-existence. Returned to the Italians in the 1950's, the city's inhabitants are now mostly Italian, the Slavs live in the hills above the city.

The telephone directory of Trieste still holds the most remarkable mixture of surnames from all around Europe.

The Joyce school has been running for twenty years now. Joyce scholars from all around the world are sitting around the table in the open air at night. There are three young women from Teheran, who tell us how wonderful it feels to spend a week without wearing a hijab, they will have to put them back on again as soon as they go home. There are scholars from Serbia, from Russia, from the USA. I get talking to Laura Peleschiar, the director of the Joyce School and she gives me a personal story which perhaps coincides with what fascinated Joyce so much about the tiered ethnic components of the city. Her mother's maiden name was Stella Lussi. It's a typical Italian name, she says. When her mother was dying some years ago and she went to visit her in the hospital, she discovered a new name on the medical chart at the foot of the bed. The hospital staff had put down her mother's maiden name as Luxic, a typical Slovenian name. It turned out that her mother had hidden her Slav identity all those years. Not only that, Laura discovered that her mother's first name was originally Stalina, after Stalin, which was then converted to the more Italian name Stella.

This kind of hidden identity is familiar to me. I met a woman from Dublin recently whose father was German but that fact was kept from her until she once accidentally found a letter addressed to his former German name. For a large part of my life I did everything to conceal my German identity. I tried my best to be as Irish as possible. The Irish language doesn't make you more Irish, it is the haunting ghost Irishness of the past. I'm not sure I ever got the hang of being properly Irish, it's the hardest thing. Being Irish is not something you can acquire. Wearing something green on Saint Patrick's day or singing 'Dublin in the rare old times' doesn't do it. Your identity is not like a T-shirt you can put on. It's not an address or a passport or any amount of cultural posturing, it is more like a space in between, a memory you have fallen into and cannot get out of.

Are the Irish different? Why do we keep asking ourselves that question? Is it the fear of mixture? Is it the fear of being like everyone else? Is it the fear of disappearing in the lake of global capitalism that now sends us all back to the protection of our local identities?

One of the Joyce scholars had gone to live in England for most of his life and has now returned to live in Ireland, just outside Limerick, but they won't let him be Irish. His own family won't even allow him to come back as a fully Irish person, he's gone too British for them, he's become a stranger, he's lost his accent and will never quite be allowed to return. When we talk about migration in Ireland we seem to think of nothing but outward migration, we don't count inward migration as being the same thing in reverse. We call ourselves generation emigration, we don't call ourselves generation immigration.

For all these reasons, we must admire Joyce for flying outwards into exile, away from the Irish nets which threatened to confine him inside a single culture and led him to look back and create the figure of Bloom, the man who belongs and doesn't belong.

Around the table on a warm evening in Trieste, the scholars are all trying to avoid talking about Brexit. It is the big subject now. Everyone is in shock at the British decision to leave the European Union. Britain of all countries, the place of such great cultural freedom, is now in the process of going backwards in time. Nobody wants to believe it is going to happen. It seems irrational that any country can take on such a narrow national position in a world that is post-national? How can any country, in the twenty first century, become so afraid of the global condition to follow nativist ideals of purity? There is no value in purity, we have long gone past that kind of thing in Europe.

One of the Joyce scholars mentions that he was listening in to the BBC this morning for the latest news on Brexit and heard instead a moment's silence for the Battle of the Somme. It seems quite remarkable that this exit from the European Union comes slap on time, a hundred years after the Somme, a hundred years after Ireland began to exit the British Empire with the Proclamation. Britain has been holding on to that First World War tragedy as a deeply British event, unable to hand over to a collective European grief. It is the hardest thing, to step outside private national sorrow, to mourn together with your former enemies across the trenches. It seems like a breakthrough that the Irish have invested so much over the past decades into that idea of collective grief, not only for the heroes of 1916 but also those who fought for the British Empire in the First World War.

It is liberating in this moment when Britain wishes to leave the European Union, to remember a moment of great humanity across the battleground of Europe – the story of a British soldier at the Somme who stood tall and walked out into the firing line to save a wounded comrade who had been screaming for hours, trapped on the barbed wire. The soldier found the German guns going silent while he carried out this brave rescue of a friend. We hold out for these bits of collective humanity. We see the gift of friendship and open borders. We see the dangers of falling back into isolation and nationalism.

On the street outside the restaurant in Trieste, a woman begins singing. She wears a long colourful dress, she has bright red lipstick on, long earrings and a straw hat with the rim turned up. She has a great voice. Her strumming on the guitar is more like Talking Heads, even though the song she sings is traditional. I can make out the word 'Corazon'. She is singing in Spanish, not Italian. We ask her where she is from.

Gitano she answers.

Gitano, from where?

Everywhere, she says.

She waves her hand and gives a great smile, a flash of gold. She is happy with her answer, happy to be a *Gitano*, the Spanish for gypsy, happy not to belong anywhere more specific than to the people she comes from, the memory of her ancestors, happy not being pinned down to any region, any city, any nation, any fixed place of origin.

All the wars of the twentieth century were in some way about the idea of home and nationhood and people forced from their homes. We have now entered into this new world in which home is no longer a fixed place. We are all on the move. We have gone beyond those strict rules of belonging for which we fought so bitterly in the past. Home used to be something we were conscripted into from birth, a place you declared allegiance to in some form or another, a place you would give your life for, a place to die for. Now we wake up in this new century of migration to find ourselves facing up to the fact that home is something more fluid, something from which we may be set adrift.

We are from everywhere. We are from anywhere. We are what we sing for.

So here is what I want to do –

It would be great to get the 1916 Proclamation read out on Moore Street, right on the street where the revolutionaries were forced to hand over their letter of surrender. All the people on Moore Street, wherever they come from, would read the document out, each person repeating a tiny fragment, have the whole thing filmed, put the fragments together in a kind of installation which would then be repeated on an endless loop on a screen, maybe as part of one of the permanent commemorative exhibitions.

The Proclamation, reclaimed by the people of Ireland in 2016 – the citizens, the inhabitants, the visitors, the strangers, the stayers and the returnees, the non-residents, the non-nationals, the non-Irish, everyone present on the street in one day, reading out their proclamation in all the voices of the world.

You would have the woman selling bananas beginning with the words – 'Irishmen and Irish women'. You would have the man from Bengal selling sugar cane saying – 'in the name of the dead generations'. You would have the woman in the long blue African dress saying – 'strikes for her freedom'. You would have a group of schoolgirls on their way home giggling as they repeat the word – 'freedom'.

You would have a series of white cards held up one by one with the words of the Proclamation written in small bite-sized sections. You would throw each card away into the street as the words have been spoken, like Bob Dylan does on 'Subterranean Homesick Blues'.

You would have the woman with the brown headscarf saying – 'cherish the children of the nation equally'.

Yes – you would have that phrase repeated over and over, you like it so much. Say it again – cherish. There would be a line-up of people waiting to say it. You would have the word echoing all around the city in the voices of Chinese men and Malaysian women. The woman in Anne's hot bread shop would say it and then ask you, what is it for, love? You would have the man sitting on his stool holding the *cash-4-gold* sign saying it like it was the password to some secret bank account. The man selling the green bananas from Kenya will give the word a great musical twist. Cherish in a Polish voice. Cherish in a Vietnamese voice. Cherish with a German roll outside Lidl. Cherish like Scottish, like English, like Irish. The women selling contraband cigarettes would come in with a further echo, crying the word out along the street like it was the most exotic new fruit of all time and can only be sold on the black market –

Cherish, cherish, cherish…

Mise Éire:
Sine mé ná an Chailleach Bhéarra

Mór mo ghlóir:
Mé a rug Cú Chulainn cróga.

Leanne O'Sullivan

As a child I was fortunate to have had as my teacher the local genealogist who was also a historian and musician. Whenever there was a chance and good weather we took our school work outdoors and learned, through his storytelling and memory, about the place. There were nature walks, history walks, music and verse. This was a classroom where we learned the names of our townlands, translating the Anglicized sounds into Irish and back again into the familiar mirror world of our English where we could know the place in a different way – every possible description of a field or hillside you could dream up: breac, seiscan, sceach, ard, mín gallán, lios, sí; speckled, marshy, hawthorn, high, smooth, standing stone, fort, the fairies. On the walks we would be so much in awe of the stories he told us – stories about the Cailleach Bhéarra who had her seat in Ballycrovane Harbour, not far from us;

the Children of Lir whose gravesite was in the next Parish; Old Donn who minded the gateway to the underworld out on the Bull Rock; about how our people survived the famine, survived evictions (neighbours building a new home – *this* home – for an evicted family in one night) – 'mythology' could almost be co-terminus with 'history' and vice versa. As children, how could we tell the difference? Sometimes there was a sense of a chronology, but mostly these events seemed to happen in the general not-so-distant past. And all of these stories were about giants and transformations, about larger than life characters and triumph over adversity – and it all happened in Beara – we were in the midst of it, full of wonder and awe!

And of course I learned, along with all my classmates, about the great heroes and heroines of the Easter Rising – about the miscommunication, the taking of the GPO, and about the execution of those big men in Kilmainham Gaol. Their names – Clarke, Connolly, McDiarmada, Plunkett, Ceannt, McDonagh and Pearse – became embedded in the firmament that upheld other prodigious heroes, even those as huge and unimaginable as Cú Chulainn, Finn Mac Cumhal, Oisín, the almost Gods. Of course we knew the men of 1916 were historical figures, but the sense of timelessness and 'appointment' was implicit in the language of the Proclamation that was read to us – 'the dead generations', 'the old traditions', Ireland's 'exiled children' and it's 'exaltation among the nations' – an air in the language that we had become almost numbed to at Mass – but we recognised it when we heard it, and without realising it understood the kind of rhetoric that could drop fire in the soul.

But there was one other man who was just as important to us Béarrachs – who as children we imagined being as much of a hero as all the others. The man who we believed must have influenced and inspired Padraig Pearse as much as any other revolutionary – Pádraig O'Laoire, born and bred in Eyeries on the Beara Peninsula, was the very man who taught Pearse Irish when he was a young schoolboy, who told him about the old Cailleach and who undoubtedly inspired one of our island's greatest poems, Mise Éire. Could you beat that? The Cailleach, who would 'sweep us away' like any mean old witch if we were bold children, inspiring Padraig Pearse and the 1916 Rising. And a local Beara man in the middle of it. How wonderful to know that an ordinary man or woman could walk into a legend and become part of it.

I was reminded of this symbiotic relationship between myth and history recently, when Padraig Harrington, whose family are from Eyeries, made a trip down from Dublin to his father's homeplace near the village, and a neighbour's child, when she heard of his visit, responded with – 'Oh! Padraig Harrington! Who was shot in the Rising!'

In the very flesh.

And there was a well below the sea, and the nine hazels of wisdom grew there. Their leaves and blossoms broke within the same hour and fell in a shower that raised a purple wave. And the five salmon that were waiting there ate the nuts so that their scales glowed brighter with their magic. They swam to the seven rivers of wisdom that sprung up from the well. If someone were to eat one of those salmon they would devour all the knowledge of the world. That was the story, how it was told, in the hundred fire-lit homes, the smuggling in of myth.

The Republic guarantees religious and civil liberty, equal rights and equal opportunities to all its citizens, and declares its resolve to pursue the happiness and prosperity of the whole nation and of all its parts … oblivious of the differences carefully fostered by an alien Government, which have divided a minority from the majority in the past.

But what can myth really do? Does it always have the potential to inflame every soul that comes across it? What stories might begin to offer light and insight to a generation of Irish people who have lost their homes, or who have had to leave home, or those who struggle to find in the daily newspapers the Ireland they were promised? Is this a country where both religious and civil liberties can exist harmoniously and side-by-side?

❧

At the landing for the cable car that will bring you across to Dursey Island from the Beara mainland is the typical cluster of charming chaos that is Irish road signage. However, this particular cluster is a little different than most – there is a sign for Moscow (3310KM), New York (4860KM), The Beara Way (all directions), and Tír na nÓg (25KM). Though Tír na nÓg was very rarely spotted by anyone from the Beara Peninsula, New York always felt like the more mythological destination – the city that fostered and sometimes vanished so many of our relatives, full of bright lights, differences, and possibility. Perhaps Oisín would have fared better there, would have survived the rough and ready 'New York minute' more satisfactorily than he did the idyllic years he spent in the land of forever.

Can you really go home again? Is there a place for the hero in the real, ordinary, up and at it world? And if you are different – if you are the kind of hero that is here to speak up for difference, is the path you take in the pursuit of happiness going be troubled, troublesome and yet absolutely essential?

There is a great joy in loving your home place, its people, in loving the life you have. It is so tempting to turn a blind eye, to look away and try to escape the necessary pain of growth. When the disenchanted Oisín returned to Ireland it was not the place he had known before. His comrades were nowhere in sight, the people were enthralled to a power totally alien to the one he had known. It was not the land of heroes that he had left behind and it was more than he could physically bear.

But as a young person fascinated by story I didn't understand most of these subtleties and nuances – or if I did I didn't care. Standing on top of what we call The Mining Road, looking down at the Cailleach, Teach Donn and the Children of Lir; at the great Atlantic and the mountains still pouring little rivers of copper, I felt all at once wonderfully tiny and also caught in a great light. I thought I could see the whole world – that I could step right into it and do anything – could come to the edge of the world and not fall off.

THE CAILLEACH TO THE HERO

'Stranger, I can tell you no new thing.
The way into darkness is open –

all day and all night old Donn holds watch
on the deep Atlantic where the dead assemble,
on an island rock hewn into a cavern
that's open end to end and shines like gold
when sunlight passes through. There the birds

flying in over the rock bring him sweat meal,
and the whole island is bathed in that essence.
When the light of the setting sun pierces
the cave and is cast along the water
then the road between the living and the dead

lies open, until the sun falls again below
the earth and disappears. And this is night,
though it has a darkness that is slight
and a twilight glimmering from the west.
You will see, the way down is easy –

lowlands of the earth and man's deepest self,
the poisons, the waste and debris of this world
you will meet without difficulty, and
although you will be alive you will be dead,
you will have the look of death like the others,

for all those others who have spoken for you here.
But if you decide to retrace your steps,
to bring yourself back to the world you came from
do it quickly, and leave nothing behind.
It is never enough to return as a mere shadow

in the flame, a likeness longing to speak.

But to return, to feel your whole self kicking
and gasping, to cry out loud and clear from
the shoreline, body and soul intact, believe me,
that is the real labour, that will be your work.'

BIG HOUSE

Now they are gathering in the field –
that's my neighbour standing
shawled amongst them, dressed in black
and facing the heavy frame of a doorway.

Last week I stood waist-deep in the water
and watched the villagers take pieces of drift
from the strand, their palms and elbows
full of stones that shone like newborn faces.

They were building this, large house
and a dark door facing the ocean.

❦

The sky passes over like a grey animal
and in the distance I can smell the rain coming.
I wonder do they notice, or do they feel the cold.

They are opening the doors now and begin to flow,
one long line, into its stomach. I follow,
a soundless shell, moved by something I can't name.

They are solemn and clasping their hands,
wrapped up in themselves like sleeping birds.

The chill settles on my throat. I am a stranger here,
a mind barren among these others.

My eyes are moving like a baby's hand among
the salt hardened stones, the mouth-flame of candles.

There's the man that lead us in; gliding up
the middle passage, bodiless under all those robes,
with crests of gold embroidery rising with his lungs.

His breath flickers on the candles, stretching their light
to every corner, and for a moment there is a gathering of eyes.

❧

When I leave I will take this with me – death and life
sweating in the stones, and that untouchable light.

I am alone with these breathing heads, staring at the stones,
the moist spots of ocean I touched before.

I remember the lightening white of waves,
that fragrant moan I slept with as a child,

letting my head sway in its lap, and breathe in
what I breathed there once.

❧

The room makes one deep sound
like curraghs swaying together.

The man at the table is speaking – he speaks
but the ocean comes to my ears.

When the people kneel,
I kneel with them, trembling.

When they sing I bow my head,
unhook the spade of my tongue
and mouth my silences.

OISÍN

He hesitates before taking Niamh's hand.
The water is glittering. His horse
is ready, restless in the morning light.
He stands on the wide, white shore,
looking back at the home-place
for the last time. He knows the story
will change in him as time passes,
no matter how well he has learned it,
no matter how well he was taught.
Love and grief. Weeping and singing.
Believing there was magic in the stones.
Mountains and rites and sovereignty.
Always with loss to come, and growing
tired among the heather and vetch.
Still, he thinks, what times we saw,
what astonishment! He keeps trying
to taste that wholeness but cannot.
No matter, he says, looking out towards
the ocean. It is almost spring again.
Tomorrow I will be living on the island,
laughter and birdsong clear from the shore,
sunlight giving way to coolness at night.
I will have fine things, he says, and perfect skies.

EUMNESTES

When I arrived in this country for the first time
I had in my possession only one book,

and being almost completely alone wrote
in such detail everything I could remember

                                          – the big bang,

the years of Nestor, the great disasters
and disturbances of weather; world ending

and world beginning, blue unto great darkness
unto blue again; unto temples and courtyards,

unto kingdoms and faltering customs.
Not that I fully understood, but in this way

I have been useful, have minded how they lived,
how they harvested cotton and grain,

what seed caught in the amber drop.

How once a man might have luckily sensed
the danger meant for him, something creeping

in the great, dark expanse, just before he decided
to turn around and come back, find another way.

How he must have listened closely, watched
for signs, for trails, or deciphered how a peal

of light falling through the trees could mark
roughly a way in, the way out again,

so that he knew the path in the future must be –
which is the reading I try to bear in mind.

And though I am from a place that is full of story and
history, there is a huge silence that sits in the landscape. I
couldn't count how many times I asked my Grandmother
to tell me about her family's involvement in the IRB or
in that Easter Weekend, and every time I was met with
silence. I always wondered if this silence could be two-fold
– a fear of telling too much, and also a sort of reverence for
such a large, weighty past and its traumas. In Beara, and
I believe in Ireland in general, there is still a deep respect
for the invisible world – places where things happened or
where presences reside, and even if you never saw them
you could not help but believe in their facticity. According
to Liam O'Dwyer's study, Beara in Irish History, there
are 284 circular forts on the peninsula; 199 burial gallans,
15 wedge graves, 11 mass graves, 17 stone circles, twenty
folacht bhiaidh, 18 bullans, 9 portico graves and 24 ancient
habitation caves in the mountains and, whether ignored
or revered, these are all for the most part left alone by the
human population. Indeed, the Cailleach, standing stones,

gravesites and other landmarks are usually left to the elements in Beara, mown around, excluded from maps – not ignored, but regarded with suspicion and superstition. It's a matter of minding your own business and whatever spirit is in the place will do the same.

At school we learned something of what those places meant literally and imaginatively, in terms of topography, family and ritual. The often supernatural or mythological narratives encoded and fleshed out, if you like, the physical qualities of the landscape. The wariness we had about the old Hag of Beara – and the rock that sits silently in the harbour, that is supposed to be her petrified remains meant that Beara's mythology was never something fossilized or hermetically sealed, locked away in an old museum cabinet. Stories about her were always being told and re-cast and then put away. Gallans that fall into the earth and that are found again years later when the spade hits the stone keep broadcasting their stories across the whole place. This cycle of loss and renewal means that these rocks have come to represent something other than a 365 million-year-old landscape that shapeshifts in fits and starts over the plates and fault lines that are our foundations. The remains of the Cailleach, along with the other standing stones and stone circles (known locally as fairy forts) that populate the area communicate something beyond themselves – regeneration, endurance, imagination – and without those fault lines they would not exist.

THE CAILLEACH TO THE WIDOW

(after Lucille Clifton)

Fair? Don't talk to me about fair.
When I came to the river in spate
I could only carry one of my two
companions across it with me,
tucking him safely under my arm,
leaving the other trembling behind us
in the dark, casting his profanities.

But let those things stay unreconciled.
How they bewitch you into thinking
everything can be saved.
But that is not what you want.
You want to save only what you love,
which is a form of suffering,
immaculate, leaving no scar.

But you know this already,
as you hold your arms out toward
the other shore, still determined
to make any bargain, to grasp what's
left of the world you came from,
the light failing fast, the waters
rising quickly around you.

PROCLAMATION

Now, an old truth rises to its zenith
in my adult life, a tide at sunset suddenly
filling the glooming light. Or perhaps
I hear the midnight prowl of my father's
mother swaying through my head,
repeating news of sickness or of death;

how she'd take the *Book of The Ancestors*
under the soft pelt of her elbow,
ascend the landing in her nightdress
and disappear with a labouring fullness
into the moth-pink light of her bedroom,
rooting out relations, muttering her own

continual augury, her common-sense portent.
I almost didn't believe when she herself
was gone, and we sat around her chair
that morning after, until someone said it,
     finally – *tiocfaidh an lá,*
my glimmerwoman of the small hours.

PUXLEY CASTLE, DUNBOY

'…being forever in the pre-trembling of a house that falls.'
Galway Kinnell

Only toe the ash now,
remembering how they've cleared it,
raised it,
roofed away the vaulting birds
and winter's cobbled underthings,

glassed up the eyeholes and the brow –
just toe the ash now.
A sea swims again
in her grey face
and melts the quarrel of the fire.

I'll mind an old familiar sky
and starlings banking in the eaves;
words I'll keep like *dungeon, turret* –
What city in the trees?
Whose barbed chiming weeds?

And these old purses
hatching through the dawn?
I'll mind an uncle who comes striding
from the fires. Oh boys, says he,
We're all a sea door down.

HEIRLOOM

A penny dropped
a hundred years ago
turns up beneath
our sweetheart cabbage,

but Love, we are still
out for spring roots,
honeyed wets
and their vanished tracks.

'Cherishing all of the children of the nation equally'

A place becomes muscular when we give it dramatic purchase, recreate it through matter and memory. In fact, it tells us more about our present selves, our imaginations, and how we think about our origins and our ends. The mythologies we build around our fears and identities endure in the landscape and weather the test of superstition. If we wandered too far, the Cailleach was sure to sweep us away or turn us into animals. She had stolen a Bible from Saint Caitairn who in anger turned her stone as she tried to escape by leaping across Coulagh Bay. In our world, the Cailleach was alive and kicking and out for mischief, and her incarnations as a hare, bean feasa or healer woman, or a fairy woman were too familiar to resist the appeal to the imagination. The body of the Cailleach might have been fossilized but her spirit was irrepressible. Our experience of her was everywhere. She had carried rocks and stones in her apron and set them down in piles along the coast, and these are our mountains. She hauled Scariff Island into Coulagh Bay as a birthday present to herself. The standing stone on the top of Bere Island was the one she used to kill a woman who had offended her. These supposedly inanimate features in the Beara countryside have been characters in some of the best theatre I've ever seen.

These were mostly stories to entertain and threaten children. But it doesn't take long to understand how stories about the Cailleach came out of an insecure and reactionary Catholic tradition that encouraged suspicion of the feminine and kept her separate and outside of the stone boundaries of the church. The Cailleach had originally been a pre-Christian sovereignty goddess, but much of her power was diminished when pagan belief collided with Catholic orthodoxy. Of course, this image of an earth goddess, goddess of harvest and creation, came to me later through reading, as my own interest in the place became something distinct from my affection and sense of home. The tension between the two characters of the Cailleach – one sensual and creative, the other a witch and hag-like – was exactly what was needed to spark a stance my poetry. I began to write poems about the woman herself, finding in her the potential of my own mother, grandmothers, and myself.

It is by way of these tensions and conflicts that local people have adapted the way they interact with parts of the landscape, shifting our perception of the place and revising – 're-membering' – the boundaries that contain it and keep us safe. Well outside of the sanctified walls of the church and its burial grounds, there is a sense of the sacred, and if not the sacred then of the intuited. Not far from where the Cailleach made her leap across Coulagh Bay there is a cillíneach, or killeenagh, an old burial ground where infants who died before they were baptised were interred. Because they had not been initiated into the Catholic tradition they were not allowed to be buried within the consecrated ground adjoining the church. Instead, parents took the remains to liminal sites: corners of fields, disused buildings. It is incredibly moving to visit these burial sites, almost completely hidden, and the graves themselves unmarked except for slabs of rugged, unworked rock. And what is particularly moving about this and other cillíneachs in the area is that they are usually founded on or near sites of older or ancient significance. For example, the site of the cillíneach near my homeplace was also an eighth- or ninth-century monastic settlement. Several standing stones are nearby. Bishop Dive Downes describes the site in Coulagh as a ruin during his visit to the area in 1699 and 1700, implicating a continuity and a foundation for a community who relied on their sense of *the* place, rather than non-specific 'sense of place,' to steady them. These burial grounds are now tended by both kindness and anxiety. We often talk about the comfort in having somewhere to visit when a loved one has passed away; but we are made uneasy when we think of where the supposedly 'wingless' souls of these children went– into limbo, space, open air, places with no boundaries. I will never forget hearing the voice of a mother of one of the children who was buried in a cillíneach, at the time when the Vatican were considering dropping limbo as a point of destination for uninitiated souls. The grief in her voice was unbearable – where was her child, she asked, if even this 'nowhere' no longer exists?

Although it was no answer, I felt a glimmer of hope to know that close to the cillíneach in Coulagh, and within the boundaries of the old monastic site, is the stone formation known as the Hag's footprint – made at the very moment she leapt away from that almost forgotten emissary of the Catholic Church – just before she was turned to stone herself, a symbol of endurance and absolute steadiness in the landscape.

SAFE HOUSE

When they were beginning to build a country
some of the men came to hide in a house
where there was a family, and a child upstairs,
listening. They told him what to say if anyone

ever asked. Say they were never there.
Say there was only a family in that house.
And during the night the boy went to the room
where their bags and belongings were hidden.

He felt along the canvases, the mouldy wet
and sag of the straps. His fingers touched on
papers and coins, and lifted out the revolver,
its coolness and the weight of it in his hands.

Then he felt nothing. His blood crept slowly
and dark along the floorboards, underneath them,
and the room shook, and stood still,
and seemed to hang for a moment in that night.

When they found him they cleaned him,
his face, gently and quickly, and his mother
wrapped him in a blanket and took him
out to a corner of the farm and buried him.

Back in the house they gathered his things,
and built up a fire again in the kitchen,
burning his clothes, his shoes, all the signs
and small, clumsy turnings of a child.

And afterwards, in the freezing dark, the father
went out to find the doctor and the parish priest
to tell them what had happened, and what they
should say if anyone ever asked.

Tell them there was never a child.
Say they were never there.
There was never a home
or the found, easy measures of a family.

There was never a map that could lead back to
or out of that place, foreknown or imagined,
where the furze, the dark-rooted vetch, turned
over and over with the old ground and disappeared.

CHILDREN OF THE CILLÍNACH

Come to us with lilies and meadowsweet,
come to us by heart and not by sight,
that heaving of love which aches still,
coffined in your belly's darkening loam.

Mother, I've known your weight
and the length of your soft hands
bent over this rugged, unworked soil.
I've known you by the forgetful daisies

strung with blue and red twine.
I open my eyes; you are watching me.
If ever I am allowed a voice
you will know me when I speak:

if I were unwinged in nothingness I would
bring home to you a memory of wings.
The scythe which undercuts life I remember,
and above, a chorus of birds, the petals

of daisies lifting. Hear me;
I will know you again among the crickets
and billowing trees. We will survive the earth.
Are you not my mother?

Was it not you I heard in the thrashing dark?
The one whose hands
I felt unbury me and baptise my soul
in a fountaining of tears?

And still I love this country

In Beara a townland could be a small division of land with just a few houses or it could be the size of a village. Many of the boundaries that divide the townlands are made by the streams that run down from the mountains.

I love how those boundaries were kept moveable and unsafe by the coppery-red water that flowed over ground and underground, streams that swelled to bursting and sometimes – rarely – came close to disappearing. I loved how easily I could find them if I listened.

The first time I took my husband, Andrew, for a walk around the townlands near Eyeries he kept asking, How do you know where we are when there aren't any signs, even on the map?

I just knew. A map in the memory, a constellation underfoot and on the tongue; the field, hillside or stone in the meaning to prove it; the beginning of another farm; the sound of water orientating me. And all of it shape-shifting, transformative, magic.

In one of the roofless, pre-famine stone ruins that we passed, in the townland of Gorth, there once lived a man known locally as Willie the Goat, for the simple reason that he used to keep a goat in his house. I wonder sometimes how time will transform or 're-member' – in a sense, re-assemble – the mocked and teased figure of Willie, if our tradition of myth-making and hero-making will have done its redemptive work so that in fifty or a hundred years' time the old Gorth village is still somewhere children are warned away from for fear of Willie who has become half-man, half-goat, a huge satyr eyeing passers-by from one of those abandoned homes that would still survive, overgrown but perfectly dependable as a place full of possibility and imagination in the old village.

LABHRAIDH LOINGSEACH

To chance upon him – your first confessor
for so many years, low to the ground,
his bare-breasted stare all eyes and ears,
and himself confessing without a sound;

to admit him from within, then look again
to the wing-span of his arms, the subtle
pounding of his temples that seems to turn
and burn through what he would conceal –

drawing out his animal ears, that animal life.
He stirs a syllable in the air
like an old willow whose song might hook you,
or cast your features in such relief.

Now you see that nothing else can happen:
this body, this weight breaks kindly open.

We pledge our lives to the cause of its freedom and its welfare

❧

Once, on another trip to the see his in-laws,
Andrew asked me who lives in a house that
was clearly empty, boarded up. I replied with
an evasive quickness, an answer inherited and
taken for granted:

– The person who lives there goes to work
sometimes in England.

For years, I imagined this neighbour and others working, as
my grandfather had worked years ago, for contractors such
as McAlpine's Fusiliers, with their builder's gait kept steady
and stooped to make ends meet. As I got older I learned very
clearly what 'England,' in this case, stood for; it was the local
way of saying, without saying, that our neighbour had been
admitted to a special type of hospital, the kind of which was
too shameful to utter.

But these days I can say it a bit more easily – because
when I was younger the boundaries and lines of perception
in my own life and mind burst their banks, disappeared;
so that when I became too unwell to take care of myself I
walked – or, rather, was led – into a that special place that,
thankfully, had very firm boundaries, very real locks and a
wonderfully mundane and predictable routine, provided for
me, in Shakespeare's phrase 'for thine especial safety.'

As the days and weeks and months of hospitalization went

by, I became aware that I, too, had taken, as if in my sleep, some rhetorical ferry across the Irish Sea. I met neighbours and acquaintances who had disappeared to 'England.' They would come through the hospital's revolving doors, out of their minds or unspeakably depressed, and go through the script we all had become used to: quick promises never to say we saw each other, never to talk about it at home. At night we would watch the news, take our medications, say goodnight and go to bed with the peacocks wailing all through the darkness next door.

It was because of that experience – and my own efforts to haul myself back into the knowable, workable world – that I began to find usefulness in the stories I grew up with. Until then I was just merely fascinated by the giants and the heroes, the mystical mythical lands and the dream of brighter lights. But it was during this time of breaking apart that I realised how myth could actually be a sort of grammar – a way of narrating or reading the world so that we might come to some kind of truth, a truth that is embedded deeply in our human consciousness and that we share with each other.

Perhaps the kernel of truth is just that: before medication or maps or theology or logic, we told each other stories to make sense of our experiences, to provide a map that had a beginning, a middle, and an end. And that the heroes are still here – perhaps they never went away – and that if we can't always be one, that we must be ready to look out for them.

The necessity of these old stories suddenly began to make sense to me then, and when a friend came to visit me and reminded of this old piseóg, I was ready to hear it: that a person shouldn't walk into the middle of a fairy fort at night.

If you do, the fairies work their mischief and move the stones around to confuse you. They shift the boundaries of the field you came in by, lock the gate, grow the grass ten feet higher, turn the place on its head. And there is only one cure for it: to cross a fairy fort at night you must turn your coat inside out – you must change the way you are in the place, shift your perspective, open the gate, free yourself – let yourself out.

MAN ENGINE
Trial

The blast
travels upwards,
inwards
and out of sight.

Cnoc Rua –
the old route
re-shapes itself
at your feet,

welds into
the crooked stair
of the shaft.
The engine roar

that ferries
you down
shudders and gives
like any landing place,

any last held
breath
your lungs
have drawn.

Breathe,
breathe
into the heart
of it again –

Candlelight

– into the cankerhole,
the glandular dark.
Down
and down

between the burst
and deafening black.
I am always
looking back.

My own shape
in the foul air
marks the spot
where I stopped

to shield my eyes,
all the light
repealed
by clouds

of dust and ash –
but here I almost see,
can just make out
by candlelight,

at the end of the level,
a softer gold
and yellow glimmer
in the white quartz lode.

Tommyknockers

Small rappings
in the lode,
dark fluttering
across the beams.

It could be
a shiver in the earth
or a warning call
raised,

their knuckles
panic white,
timbers rasping
in their hold.

Or a tap
on my shoulder
pelting
to a stream.

Listen the glut,
the first scree
howling down
the shaft.

Listen
the mouths
that lie foul
in the water.

Sea Level

We always knew
they were mining
below the sea,
under the great bellies

of the earth –
could hear sometimes
far out
beyond the pier

the inconsolable
hammering
of those workers
ossify in the tides,

the fill
of their shovels
streaming above them
in candlelight

towards crescent moon
or starfish,
where I wade
in the grey water,

the drag of my feet
hauling clouds
of shingle and ore
along their dressing floors.

Ascent

Perhaps this is why
I keep returning –
the dark
always ascending

and the light
retreating softly
beyond the shaft.
At nightfall

the engine hauls
you back
in ones and twos,
up past

the darkened galleries,
the sunk
knowledge
and wet quartz

blasted
and glittering among
the constellations –
starlight,

your own name
called out,
your hands entering
the world again.

THE WATCHMAN

'..and now I watch for the light, for the signal fire'
(Agamemnon trans. Robert Fagles)

Oh Lord, grant me tonight my clearest sight
and compass my watch with a steady eye
for fear I dream I'm swept away this time.

I saw the bright millstone lower again to the sea
and the stars telling our fortunes in a gaining wind —
friends who've fallen on the way, ambition, envy,

too much dreaming. How shall I keep staying?
In the middle of the longest night I woke trembling
on the staff of my elbows but recognised enough

to make my living real: a foothold in the earth,
my grove against the currents and those cold,
Martello fires, our great, silent heralds of the sky.

Nothing happened but the dark, the skin
of the dark repeating,
       Shake yourself, Sentry.
Look alive.

The Republic in Dreamtime

Theo Dorgan

In our time, in general political discourse, the term 'Republic' has acquired a comet's tail of meanings, clarifications, propositions and counter-propositions, some founded in philosophical enquiry, others deriving from the cultures and practices of what we might call 'actually existing republics', so much so that it would be a brave poet, historian or lexicographer who ventured an encompassing definition at the present moment.

In the Irish political context, the term carries a cloudy freight of half-understood meanings, and in our general political life has only rarely been subjected to rigorous analysis. This has been a problem since the foundation of the Free State, indeed since that moment when the seven signatories declared Ireland a Republic and none, except Connolly, had anything but a vague idea of what a Republic was, or should be.

Not the least of the peculiarities of Ireland as Republic is that nowhere in our Constitution do we declare ourselves a Republic, with the inevitable consequence that there are no articulated republican values in the fundamental document that grounds our laws and our social being.

A part-consequence of this neglect, this bizarre omission, is that the term 'Republican' has been annexed over time by a significant cohort that fundamentally opposes itself to the legitimacy of the actual Republic in which we live, on the grounds that they, and they only, are the legitimate inheritors of the only declared Republic.

As is all too common in Irish politics, there are absurdities at work here: the actually-existing but formally unclaimed Republic is at odds with the theological Republic-to-be-established. We have a Republic that decries 'Republicans', and 'Republicans' who disdain and grant only a partial legitimacy to the Republic most of us think we live in.

I take it as axiomatic that the form of polity the Irish people wish for will continue, in whatever sense we settle on, to be that of a Republic, but as things stand we have the forms of such a polity without any principles or analysis, not to speak of consensus, on which to base our understanding of what a republic actually is.

It would, I think, be helpful if we were to formally constitute ourselves as a republic, to declare ourselves a republic not just as a rhetorical statement but as a fact backed up by a comprehensive, encompassing and ambitious set of explicit values and principles.

With this in mind, some years ago I edited a volume of essays in which eight distinguished scholars and thinkers offered their thoughts on how we might best frame a new Constitution for Ireland. I called the book *Foundation Stone*[1], and gave it the subtitle *Notes Towards a Constitution for a 21st Century Republic*. My hope, and that of the contributors, was that we might make some modest contribution towards opening a debate on how we might reform, possibly rewrite, our 1937 Constitution in order to give a more adequate and generous account of how we wished to constitute ourselves as a society, the principles and precepts we desired to see underwrite our laws and our values as an evolving society.

That book, despite being widely distributed by a professional and respected publishing house, had one review, by the artist and activist Robert Ballagh, in the SIPTU newspaper, *Liberty*. One review.

> It seems we are content to live uncritically in a republic that does not declare itself a republic, and further, that even so modest an attempt as ours to open a debate about what kind of republic we might wish to be, what a republic might actually be, is of no interest to either the professional commentators or the political formations who, in varying combinations, either rule or would wish to rule our State.

It may well be that we are simply living through a period of transition, where concrete experience coupled with trial and error will be necessary before we can even frame a debate that aims to arrive at some useful working definition of a Republic, one sufficient to our actual circumstances and fit to shape, at least in the short-to-medium term, political practice in our troubled state.

Perhaps this is as it should be, because after all the roots of the word 'republic' are in the Latin words 'res publica', the public thing, itself an amorphous, shape-changing concept and one grounded in common understanding at a given moment in history rather than, as with a legal term, being strictly and severely defined.

Nevertheless, it seems reasonable that we should at the very least articulate an understanding of what we mean by, let us say, the term 'Republic of Ireland', that we should enshrine that understanding in a Constitution, and that we should consider and frame our laws in the light of what we mean by a republic constitutionally defined. I see no reason why such a definition should not be articulated in such a way as to provide for evolution in our understanding of what it means to be human together in society. It would be, I think, unwise to embark on such a process without first coming to a clear and unambiguous understanding and acceptance of fundamental human rights viewed in the most capacious and freedom-granting terms. In other words, the consensus of the given moment must be brought into balance with the most generous and just ideas of what we wish to permit ourselves and each other, how we propose to live together in mutual esteem and respect.

It is not difficult to grasp the dangers inherent in relying simply on the consensus of a given moment in order to frame laws and indeed the Constitution. It is not so long ago that in our public life women were considered second-class citizens, even by some as second-class human beings. It is not so long ago that the term 'Irish Republic' was understood to mean 'Irish Catholic Republic'. My point here is that at particular historical moments, the public consensus accepted, as an immutable given, propositions that a short time later had come to seem impossible and absurd. Consensus, indispensable as it is, needs to be constantly challenged, must be obliged to articulate and advocate for its position, just as it must be renewed and reformulated through reasoned and fair-minded debate. Considerable difficulties arise when our contemporary understanding of human rights comes into conflict with restrictive concepts embedded in our Consitution; our solution to the inevitable pressures arising has been, up to now, piecemeal adjustments to the Constitution, a process not only unsatisfactory but in some cases downright absurd.

As understood in common sense, then, the term 'republic' is best considered as fluid, reflective and aspirational, susceptible to mutation and growth, an elastic concept that at any given moment is open to challenge and re-definition. One might say the term is not just unstable, but actively protean in all the meanings of that term.

All of which said, when we use the term 'republic' we intend a generally understood approximation, something that more or less contains the ideas of equity and equality, solidarity, justice, the common good – and equally we mean something that refuses autocracy, tyranny, hereditary rule or indeed plutocracy. Not to put too fine a point on it, we expect a republic to be a state or political entity where all are considered, at least in theory, equally provided for in their persons, rights and obligations.

If we frame this discussion in terms of the two jurisdictions on this island, the picture becomes clearer. In the North, a democracy that operates under the aegis of a constitutional monarchy; in the South, a democratic state, Republican in its form, functioning as a Republic but not claiming to be such in its Constitution. In the North, a considerable population absolutely and unconditionaly unwilling to be annexed or coerced into a Republic, however defined; in the South, a population unwilling, so far, to articulate a clear vision and statement of what it would mean to be, formally and constitutionally, citizens of a republic.

Now, at the risk of simplifying things to an absurd degree, a republic is nothing more (or less) than the concrete expression of a straightforward rational proposition, that a sovereign people should be governed by consent in accordance with an agreed set of common values, expressed in a democratic process, subservient to no external or hereditary power. You cannot meaningfully have a republic where any significant body of citizens is incorporated against its will, since the foundation of all republics is the willing association of all, of each with each, in accord with an agreed set of principles. You might think, then, that the path to a united Ireland, for a republican, is both clear and obvious: first build an actual republic in the South that provides for the greatest possible individual liberty, articulates, formulates and guarantees rights, creates a social economy that is demonstrably just and progressive, promotes equality, opportunity and justice for all – and then patiently make it plain that all on the island who wish to partake of this open polity are welcome to join it. I do not say this will inevitably happen, I am unwilling even to speculate on whether or not it is likely to succeed as a strategy, but at least it is a republican strategy, since it offers voluntary allegiance as the primary, indeed the only meaningful option.

There are signs that elements, at least, in Sinn Féin are inching towards such a position, but the larger political formations show few signs, if any, of demonstrated interest in building this open vibrant, attractive Republic.

In the popular mind, the Irish Republic was declared in the Easter Week proclamation, and the key provision was the promise that the new regime would cherish all the children of the nation equally. Like most independent post-colonial peoples, we have been slow to abandon folkloric belief in our foundational moments, and I think it is beyond argument that most Irish people still consider that the fundamental compact between government and citizens rests on this promise.

Belief and trust in this promise, a promise common to many if not all states that declare themselves republics, led many to consider that because our beginnings were in the declaration of a republic, it follows that we have been since then, de facto, a republic.

Never mind that from 1922 to 1949 the 26 county state did not formally declare itself a republic. Never mind the equally discomfiting fact that the 1937 Constitution did not define the state in terms of a republic, did not declare us formally a republic and still does not describe the state, in terms of its philosophical underpinnings, as a republic. And never mind the fact that the term 'republican' has been deployed to mean 'enemy of the actually-existing state' by every government from 1922 to, one might argue, 1998.

In the face of all this, the majority of the Irish people, by which I mean here the people of the 26 counties, have always taken it for granted that we live in a republic.

A flawed republic, to be sure, uncertain and fitful in its provisons for the children of the nation, certainly not a secular republic as the French might have it, and not underscored by a bill of rights as the American republic is, but to most people a republic nonetheless.

In the dictionary senses of 'indistinct, obscure, not clearly defined' it has certainly been, and continues to be, an ambiguous republic. I want to make the argument here that the Irish people hold to the unexamined notion that our republic is actively committed to cherishing the children of the nation, that a republic, if it means anything at all, has to be so committed, and that our governing class has never subscribed to this fond delusion.

On the 21st January 1919, the Democratic Programme was laid before the 1st Dáil, proposed by General Risteárd Ó Maolchatha and unanimously adopted. Drawn up by Thomas Johnston and William O'Brien, with the active participation of Cathal O'Shannon, this programme was toned down at the last minute by Seán T. O'Kelly. Instrumentally, we must consider it as a sop to labour forces, as a quid pro quo for the Labour Party having abstained in the 1918 elections so as to give a clear field to Sinn Féin candidates. Whatever its provenance, it was unanimously adopted. The Democratic Programme can be usefully considered as a fleshing-out of the Proclamation's promise to 'cherish the children of the nation equally.' It proposed, inter alia, that 'the Nation's sovereignty extends not only to all men and women of the nation, but to all its material possessions, the Nation's soil and all its resources, all the wealth and all the wealth-producing processes' and went on to proclaim that 'all right to private property must be subordinated to the public right and welfare.' Equally radically, and in words that resonate with the after-echoes of liberté, égalité and fraternité, the Declaration stated: 'It shall be the first duty of the Government of the Republic to make provision for the physical, mental and spiritual well-being of the children, to secure that no child shall suffer hunger or cold from lack of food, clothing or shelter, but that all shall be provided with the means and facilities requisite for their proper education and training as Citizens of Free and Gaelic Ireland.' Stirring words, indeed, and remember please that the Declaration was adopted unanimously. But consider this: in proposing the Programme's adoption, General Richard Mulcahy was speaking as the TD for Clontarf, but he was also Chief of Staff of the IRA at the time. The same man would, unforgivably, order the execution of 77 prisoners during the

Civil War three years later; he went on to become leader of Fine Gael, ironically while a member of the Seanad that his lineal successor Enda Kenny recently attempted to abolish. Speaking about the Democratic Programme on RTÉ television on the 21st January 1969, Mr. Ernest Blythe, said 'I never found anybody who took the slightest interest...[it was] some sort of a hoist of a flag.' On the same programme, Seán Mac Entee said: 'We couldn't impose a quasi-socialist policy... the workers themselves wouldn't have credited your sincerity' – having prefaced this remark by saying, in effect, that an electorate of farmers would not have stood for such a Programme.

Now in the realpolitik of the day, that is at least arguably true; what is remarkable, though, is that already the emerging state class was demonstrating an attachment to power and the exercise of power that was blithely prepared to pay lip-service to republican ideals without having the slightest intention of carrying them into effect.

There was a bitter joke in the former USSR that went: 'they pretend to pay us, and we pretend to work; that way everyone is happy.' In our stalled republic, the political class has continued in the habit of pretending they mean certain things while we, the electorate, happily pretend to believe them. This corrosive ambiguity, on both sides, from the very start laid the foundations for the emergence of a disdainful state-management class of professional politicians and senior civil servants, and at the same time for mass defection from political responsibility on the part of a citizenry reduced to a rubber stamp electorate. We became an ambiguous republic, then, in the further sense of 'uncertain as to course or conduct'.

Our constant vacillation between two main parties whose distinction one from the other is arbitrary, even theological, rather than ideological, reflects and nurtures this ambiguity, allowing both governors and governed to permanently evade the all-important question: what kind of Republic do we want to be? The sidelining of the labour interest in 1918 is what allowed the emergence of the Democratic Programme; it is a bitter paradox, then, that the Labour Party, whenever admitted to government as scapegoat and camouflage for policies they could at best hope to ameliorate in some minor way, should have so signally failed to promote and advocate for, where possible advance, the spirit if not the letter of the Democratic Programme.

On the 18th January 2009, at ceremonies held to mark the 90th anniversary of the first Dáil and the adoption of the Democratic Programme, Labour Party Finance spokesperson Joan Burton said:

> The Democratic Programme outlined a set of values for an independent Ireland that are as relevant today as they were in 1919; values that successive governments have often failed to meet.

There is a kind of tragic irony at work here, a key figure in the party whose members formulated that Democratic Programme calling for the implementation of values that party would signally fail to honour in Government, as if it were not in their power to, at the very least, drive a passionate, open puiblic debate about those values.

I do not mean to single out Minister Burton, since I am a firm believer in the doctrine of collective party responsibility, and I do not suggest she was being disingenuous 7 years ago, but as we stand here and survey the ruins of our dysfunctional, ambiguous Republic, our sovereignty bartered, so many of our people driven to near despair by energetically-pursued policies of austerity, I am minded to commend to her successors in Government the following statement from the Democratic Programme:

> We declare that we desire our country to be ruled in accordance with the principles of Liberty, Equality and Justice for all, which alone can secure permanence of Government in the willing adhesion of the people.

There is nothing at all ambiguous about the warning encoded in that final clause: the right to govern depends always and only on the willing adhesion of the people.

My profound sense at this moment in our history is that we are sliding inexorably towards the withdrawal of that consent to be governed in accordance with a mutually-understood compact. Neither the first Dáil nor any Dáil since has conceived the republic in terms of the Democratic Programme, no matter how much lip service has been paid to its ethos and values, no matter how much in our naivety we have always assumed that somewhere in back of government that ethos, those values, were somehow mysteriously at work. Well, there is precious little mystery about what is happening at present: nobody now alive has seen successive governments so resolutely determined to save the apparatus of the State at the expense of the people and our actual interests. Aggregating the sum of our disaffections, and drawing from that mass of negatives a positive, it seems to me that the time has come for us, as a sovereign people, to provide for the enactment of the Democratic Programme, or some modernised restatement of it.

Realistically, I do not expect the state class to accede to this demand, which leaves us with a question that allows of no ambiguity: what is to be done?

Well, declaring ourselves a Republic in a new, fit-for-purpose Constitution would be a good start.

The appropriation of politics by a professional political class has led to, and in part relies upon, the cultivation of a sense of helplessness among ordinary citizens. We are constantly, both directly and subliminally, fed a sense that the management of public life, the mechanics of the state, the administration of government, are complex and sophisticated processes, beyond our power to understand, and therefore beyond our power to control. This learned helplessness, this deliberately-fostered sense of helplessness, has many pernicious effects, but perhaps the most poisonous of these is the sense that radical change is not possible, is no longer possible even if once it was. From there it is only a small step to the proposition, deeply internalised in many, that any possible divagation from the status quo can only be naive, highly dangerous and in any case doomed to fail.

The men and women who embarked on the Easter Rising may well have seemed politically naive to the savvy political class of the time; with the exception of Connolly, in cold retrospect, they were certainly militarily naive, and again with the exception of Connolly, they possessed neither a political programme nor an easily-articulated vision of what the Republic they so confidently declared might or should be. It was, of course, patently ridiculous to imagine that so small and so isolated a political formation could wrest Ireland from the bonds of Empire. Everyone 'knew' that it could not be done. Yet, done it was.

It was not done by force of arms, we would do well to remember that. The British armed forces in Ireland were not defeated in battle, could not have been defeated in battle, if Britain had decided to swamp the country with its very considerable army, if London had summoned the will to enforce its rule by brute force. British rule ended in Ireland, not because the armed forces of the Republic defeated the armed forces of Empire, but because the declaration of a Republic, the visible willingness of so many prepared to enter into combat, however small their actual numbers, the sense that enough was enough, all of these things undermined the will to dominion. Simply put, the people declared themselves ungovernable. Yes, of course, armed struggle played its part, but as time recedes we are able to see the relatively minor role, in itself, that armed struggle played. Far more important was the creation of an embryonic Republic, with its own finances, however pitiful, its own courts, and its own parliament. The first meeting of the First Dáil was treated by the professional political class of the day, and by the commentariat of the time, in Ireland and in Britain, as a kind of low comedy, an absurd and quixotic gesture. It is instructive to note how little time elapsed before the government in London was treating in all seriousness with that Dublin parliament.

The declaration of the Republic was an act of imagination, and we should consider very carefully how little time it took for that act of the imagination to inhabit, to announce and embody itself in, concrete form.

How little time it took to eviscerate the dream.

I have written about this more extensively in another place[2]; here I want simply to note how, driven in part by the urgent exigencies of the time and in part by self-interested manoeuvring on the part of a politically ambitious cadre, this act of imagination was hollowed out before it could find its next level of expression.

I will be forgiven, I hope, for quoting myself:

> For the vast majority of people, the harp replaced the crown on police stations and on the letterheads of the State – and that was all. There was no pretence that the State would be founded on [meaningful] consultation with the people, no attempt to conduct and direct a broad-ranging first principles public debate on what form the State should take, what values its laws and its legislature should embody and profess. The passion of revolution, such as it was, found itself quietly extinguished in a decisive manoeuvre by a managerial class already waiting and poised in the wings.

> … with residual exceptions, the architects of our new State were in the main second-generation revolutionaries. We forget or elide a simple but profound truth: the War of Independence was largely conducted by the urban and rural poor, officered and led in the main by the lower middle class. The lawgivers and managers of the new Free State were cut from a different cloth; they edged out the rough men with a practiced ease, as is always the case. First come the dreamers and poets, and the poor who do the fighting and dying; then come the smooth men, the silky and silken voiced judges and lawyers and administrators. And, of course, in back of these respectable men, the executioners when they are needed.

In time, those of the revolutionary generation who survived into politics had the hard edges sanded off them by the ceaseless murmuring abrasions of what was in essence an unaltered and seemingly insurmountable process of governance. As the Normans became *Hiberniores Hibernii*, so too the men and women who had overthrown imperial rule made themselves comfortable in the corridors and in the assured language of power. Prisoners of the unaltered and unaltering State.

There was, there remains to this day, a sense of helplessness at the heart of government. As if stasis were fore-ordained and inescapable.

In his magnificent book-length poem *The Rough Field*[3], published in 1972, John Montague sets up a kind of counterpoint to his own words, a recurring series of quotations that question and inflect his own imaginings.

Two of these are set one above the other, by way of introducing the section entitled 'Patriotic Suite', originally published by the Dolmen Press as a pamphlet in 1966:

The first is from poet and ethnic cleanser Edmund Spenser, speaking of Ireland:

> They say it is the Fatal Destiny of that land, that
> no purposes whatsoever which are meant for her
> good will prosper.

It is a perception to chill the blood, inasmuch as its prophetic power, whatever its provenance, rings as true today as it did during the barbarous Elizabethan conquest.

Spenser, who gives no authority for this fatalistic observation, was of course sent to rule over a sizable portion of the province of Munster, and did a pretty good job of ensuring that neither the good nor the people prospered under his steely eye.

The second quotation is from Friedrich Engels:

> The real aims of a revolution, those which are not illusions, are always to be realised after that revolution.

If there were revolutionary aspirations in the Rising and in the War of Independence, I would argue that they were quickly suffocated in the lore, language and precedents of that *mentalité* of governance we so easily and unquestioningly took upon ourselves.

Well, perhaps this is no more than the dialectic of history at work: first we imagine ourselves free, then we allow ourselves to be imprisoned by ourselves.

On what grounds, though, can we say that this is necessarily the end of things, that no further radical change is possible?

None, that I can see.

It is profoundly lazy of us to accept the 1937 Constitution as immutable, imperishable, possessed of some ungainsayable permanence. It is entirely possible to take stock of ourselves, to conduct an urgent, learned and, it may be, impassioned debate about this most fundamental of documents, to formulate and embrace a more just, generous and imaginative charter for ourselves as a republic.

In my Introduction to *Foundation Stone*, I wrote as follows:

> It is not just Ireland that has changed in those long turbulent decades since 1937, the whole world has

changed; new ways of thinking have emerged, new perspectives on what it is to be human, new thought, above all, on our common stewardship of our native planet home. In the decades to come, it will not be enough to construct a new Constitution for Ireland in an hermetically-sealed vacuum. We will need to consider our polity in the larger context of the European Union, in the context of our privileged membership in the club of developed countries, in the wider context of our responsibilities and our sense of ourselves in the wider human family.

And we will have to consider as a matter of increasing urgency how justice, equality and solidarity are not alone to be defined but actively to be shared with all the other polities on our beleaguered planet.

We need, above all, the courage of imagination, the nerve and verve to think differently. And, certainly, the humility and intelligence to look beyond our habitual frames of reference for inspiration.

As a spur to this, perhaps, I draw the reader's attention to the wholly new constitution adopted by Ecuador in 2008, following a comprehensive process which took no more than seven months. The Ecuadorean Constitutional Convention was charged with producing a wholly new document in that timeframe, and succeeded in producing a Constitution that is exact and severe in its formulation, while being both exhilarating, wide-ranging and in many of its aspects startlingly progressive.

We might usefully consider six Articles:

Article 281 reads:

> Food sovereignty is a strategic objective and
> an obligation of the State in order to ensure
> that persons, communities, peoples and nations
> achieve self-sufficiency with respect to healthy and
> culturally appropriate food on a permanent basis.

Among the obligations assumed by the State under this
section are:

> Strengthen the development of organizations
> and networks of producers and consumers and
> the commercialization and distribution of food to
> promote equity within rural and urban spaces.

and

> Generate just and solidarity [oriented] systems
> of distribution and commercialization of food.
> Impede monopolistic practices and any type of
> speculation with food products.

Consider the implications of a like article in a future Irish
Constitution.

Even more radically, Articles 71-74 of the new constitution
confer rights on the natural environment, what we might term
ecosystem rights, and situates the human holistically inside an
eco-political system that is both moral and intensely matter-of-
fact:

Article 71.

Nature, or Pacha Mama, where life is reproduced and occurs, has the right to integral respect for its existence and for the maintenance and regeneration of its life cycles, structure, functions and evolutionary processes.

All persons, communities, peoples and nations can call upon public authorities to enforce the rights of nature. To enforce and interpret these rights, the principles set forth in the Constitution shall be observed, as appropriate.

The State shall give incentives to natural persons and legal entities and to communities to protect nature and to promote respect for all the elements comprising an ecosystem.

Article 72.

Nature has the right to be restored. This restoration shall be apart from the obligation of the State and natural persons or legal entities to compensate individuals and communities that depend on affected natural systems.

In those cases of severe or permanent environmental impact, including those caused by the exploitation of nonrenewable natural resources, the State shall establish the most effective mechanisms to achieve the restoration and shall adopt adequate measures to eliminate or mitigate harmful environmental consequences.

Article 73.

The State shall apply preventive and restrictive measures on activities that might lead to the extinction of species, the destruction of ecosystems and the permanent alteration of natural cycles.

The introduction of organisms and organic and inorganic material that might definitively alter the nation's genetic assets is forbidden.

Article 74.

Persons, communities, peoples, and nations shall have the right to benefit from the environment and the natural wealth enabling them to enjoy the good way of living.

Environmental services shall not be subject to appropriation; their production, delivery, use and development shall be regulated by the State.

And, my final example:

Article 11.

The exercise of rights shall be governed by the following principles:

1. Rights can be exercised, promoted and enforced individually or collectively before competent authorities; these authorities shall guarantee their enforcement.

2. All persons are equal and shall enjoy the same rights, duties and opportunities. No one shall be discriminated against for reasons of ethnic belonging, place of birth, age, sex, gender identity, cultural identity, civil status, language, religion, ideology, political affiliation, legal record, socio-economic condition, migratory status, sexual orientation, health status, HIV carrier, disability, physical difference or any other distinguishing feature, whether personal or collective, temporary or permanent, which might be aimed at or result in the diminishment or annulment of recognition, enjoyment or exercise of rights. All forms of discrimination are punishable by law. The State shall adopt affirmative action measures that promote real equality for the benefit of the rights-bearers who are in a situation of inequality.

We have only to ask, what would it be to live in, to constitute ourselves as, a Republic shaped by an equal energy of the imagination, a vision particular to ourselves and our history, a vision informed by the thought of others, a vision that can, above all, be offered for sharing?

In 1897 James Connolly wote:

> The Republic I would wish our fellow-countrymen
> to set before them as their ideal should be of such
> a character that the mere mention of its name
> would at all times serve as a beacon-light to the
> oppressed of every land.[4]

In our globalized world, through the filter of the impoverished worldview available through neo-conservative discourse, this seems a laughably naïve ambition – as naïve, let us say, as to imagine that the Ireland in which our Grandmothers and Grandfathers were born could ever have hoped to be independent.

I do not think it impossible, that we in Ireland might yet constitute ourselves as a polity in such a way as to offer example, and hope, to oppressed people everywhere – to, I might point out, the vast majority of human beings now alive. But, to do that, we would have to confront a fundamental weakness in ourselves, a servile need to be governed from elsewhere, to put ourselves in thrall to an external power, together with a rather pathetic wish to identify with the major powers at, almost, any cost.

Consider the unanimity with which our three main parties consented to impose the losses of speculating European banks on the Irish people. Consider our abject unwillingness to exercise even the minimal sovereign right, I might say duty, to inspect foreign military flights when they land in our country, our surrender of a key national resource, the Corrib gas field, on the most minimal of terms – and the enthusiasm with which we set our police force to hound and harass citizens who object to this.

Our governments, the successive governments of recent

times, did not land here from Alpha Centauri, they were elected by ourselves, in their various combinations of party and interest, in free and open elections. There is a childish and infuriating tendency in Ireland to whinge about 'the Government' as if it were not we ourselves who grant government its powers and legitimacy.

If we do not have justice, equality, fair dealing, respect for all, the right to control our own bodies, the right to health, education and homes, and if we consider these reasonable aspirations, then we have to face a fundamental question: why do we keep electing governments that are, if not actively hostile to these aspirations, certainly, and slyly, determined to stifle them by strategies of indifference?

There are, of course, complicated reasons for this, not least our unwillingness to deal directly and openly with the pathology of ourselves as a post-colonial people.

The truth is, at the very moment we gained, arguably, if not our freedom then the freedom to gain our freedom, to constitute ourselves at our best, we failed; lulled by the siren songs of the Foreign and Colonial Office, bullied by a vastly superior military power, deftly manipulated by the world masters of the art of national self-interest, partitioned as India was, with as noxious a consequence, we persuaded ourselves that the hollow outward show of freedom was much the same thing as freedom in substance, and we have an enduring bad conscience about that ever since.

In our rush to identify with the rich and powerful, we have forgotten the poor of the world, those former colonial subjects with whom, if we were grown-up enough to admit it, we have far more in common than we have with the kleptocracy of the first world.

There is a great truth that is always available to anyone living under colonial domination: no matter how much you assimilate your interests to those of the ruling class, no matter how prepared to compromise you may be, you will always be on the outside, a stranger in your own land, until and unless you are prepared to claim your freedom as an absolute condition of life.

Such a claim demands that all of the conditions of personal and political life must be brought to examination, without exception. This is a very great and exhausting task, and the imperfect nature of most post-colonial states is in part explained by the premature exhaustion of those political actors most involved in the freedom struggle. This is not just an unfortunate paradox, it is a truth recognised in advance by the apparently-defeated colonial power, and used by that power to consolidate a considerable influence and benefit in the post-revolutionary period.

More, the habit of weariness, the internalization of a sense of powerlessness, may very well be carried over into the new state – as certainly seems to be the case in Ireland.

The Irish revolution, in many respects, collapsed in the intellectual stagnation ushered in by the establishment of the Free State. Lest I be misunderstood even in a small way, I wish to say here also that in the political and armed opposition to the Treaty there was an equal stagnation, a lack of new thought, a reluctance, it may be an inability, to understand that a national revolution properly considered required a great deal more than a change of emblem over the Courthouses, a change of uniform for the police.

W.B. Yeats, no friend to revolution, understood this well:

Hurrah for revolution and more cannon-shot!
A beggar upon horseback lashes a beggar on foot.
Hurrah for revolution, and cannon come again!
The beggars have changed places but the lash
goes on.

But this was neither inevitable nor predestined. The empire clawed back much of what it had seemed to lose because it was well prepared; the long struggle against Home Rule had prompted a canny assessment of how much could be ostensibly conceded, how much could be and would be in fact retained. The power of empire is a staggering thing; its lineaments endure long after the foreign colonels have gone home, to their villas by the Tiber, their bungalows in Cheltenham. These lineaments endure because empire enters into the minds and hearts of the colonised in a myriad of ways, primarily through the instruments of education, law and civil governance. This process is so totalising, so all-pervasive, that we cannot reasonably hope to undo the colonisation of our minds and habits in a first or even a second post-revolutionary generation.

I would not wish it to be thought that I am here, from the luxury of this historical remove, criticising our grandfathers and grandmothers for their lack of vision. After all, they were caught in a terrible prison of the mind, given that the schooled intelligence on which they had to rely for a political and moral compass was formed by the very system they were hoping to overthrow. It was a very rare individual indeed who could fly free of those particular nets of history, who could articulate freely an expansive vision of freedom.

The wonder is, that in the Democratic Programme of the first Dáil, preserved in the amber of history, ignored by our ruling political class since the very day it was unanimously endorsed and adopted, and long since forgotten by ourselves, we have a charter of freedom and pride in ourselves as a republic that we could have drawn on at any time since the foundation of the State, that we can still draw on today if we wish.

If we wish.

What I think of as the State Class – career politicians, the upper strata of the Civil service, the functionaries of the apparat, together with the various formations of the rich and powerful, the emissaries of international finance, and the more cynical layers of the commentariat – have no interest whatever in seeing our Republic established (re-established if you will) on the basis of a new, decisive, moral, cultural and political imagination. It is not in their interests, for instance, that we should constitutionally and legally embrace a radical option for the poor and the powerless, that we should decisively and emphatically place equity, justice, equality and access at the heart of how we define ourselves as a Republic. I have no reason whatever to believe that in these powerful formations there is the slightest will to constitute the State as a republic in the fullest and most inclusive senses of that challenging term.

It is by no means obvious, however, that there is at present anything like a broad popular will in ourselves as citizens to embark on such a radical adventure, no matter how urgently, to me self-evidently, we need to do so. If we have been failed by our political leaders, is it not also true, at least in part, that we have failed ourselves?

In a speech given at the Royal Irish Academy in late 2015, President Higgins touched, delicately it must be said, on the questions I am raising here more bluntly:[5]

One can legitimately wonder, for example, what shape would our economy and society have assumed, had our fellow citizens kept alive, during Ireland's recent economic boom, the cultural, philosophical, political and moral motivations which underpinned the Irish national revival, or the spirit of other historical movements for social and political reform such as the Cooperative Movement. How might these elements of the past now inform our vision for the future of Ireland? What should we retain and what should we discard? What is the purpose of our State?

In a subsequent speech[6], on Easter Monday 2016 as it happens, the President said this:

> Together, we have the power to realise the possibility of an inclusive future, in which we share our Republic and its opportunities with all who belong to her – both here and abroad.

I agree with the President, we have the power to realize an amplified, inclusive and equitable future in a Republic of our own making.

I believe that there are, in civil society, and even here and there in formal politics, individuals and formations capable of driving the debate and discussion out of which we might hope to build a new Republic.

Equally, I am under no illusion about this, there are powerful forces, at home and abroad, whose powers, profits and privileges would be very much at risk in such a new dispensation, and we can count on those elements to be vehement in their opposition to such a republican re-imagining.

It will be argued that the era of the nation state is over – I ask, in whose interest is it that we believe this?

It will be argued, that Republicanism is no more than nationalism – I ask, who benefits from promoting this false equivalence?

It will be argued, that we have shown ourselves unfit to govern ourselves – I ask, who, then, should govern us?

It will be argued, the task is too great, the world is grown too complicated in its interwoven systems – I ask if the task of building a sovereign Republic now is any greater, in relative terms, than striking for independence 100 years ago against a world-girdling Empire?

As ever, what holds the balance here is the popular will.

We are faced with a great and simple question: now and in time to come, who do we want to be?

Theo Dorgan
Dublin 2016

Endnotes

1   *Foundation Stone*: Notes Towards a Constitution for a 21st Century Republic. New Island, Dublin 2014.

2   'Law, Poetry and the Republic', in *Up The Republic*: *Towards a New Ireland*, Ed. Fintan O'Toole, Faber & Faber, London 2015

3   John Montague, *The Rough Field*, Dolmen Press, Dublin 1972

4   James Connolly, 'Socialism and Nationalism', in *Shan Van Vocht*, 1897

5   The speech can be found at: http://www.president.ie/en/media-library/speeches/recovering-possibilities-discovering-the-rich-promise-of-a-moral-foundation

6   To be found at http://www.president.ie/en/News/article/president-gives-an-address-at-the-live-broadcast-of-centenary

Chronosequence

Doireann Ní Ghríofa

PROCLAMATION

I.

Behind a thick layer of museum glass,
a copy of the proclamation still sits intact.

Gently lit, the paper seems cockled, thin
like seed scattered in a field of flax, its print.

Its capitals call still, to IRISHMEN AND IRISHWOMEN
in mismatched fonts, just as it did in its beginning.

From a copy gripped in Pearse's trembling fist, it was read
aloud, translated from page to mouth and shouted to the
                                                    laughing dead,

to Sackville Street's Easter strollers, the passers-by
who dawdled a while, or jeered and rolled their eyes.

Somehow, this page survived flame and bullet
to endure as an artefact in this glass cabinet.

So many of the others were destroyed: binned, torn, burned,
pinned to bombed doors, rain-soaked, gutter-churned

until only singed fragments of them
remained: an [E] from [REPUBLIC] in a dewy spider web,

a charred [her children] tucked under two blue eggs
in the twigs of a starling's nest,

a [secret revolutionary] fallen into a horse's
manger, roiled in its convulsive

oesophagus. And so, most of the copies
brought forth by each mechanical sneeze

of the printing press were lost within weeks of birth,
transformed to miniscule flecks of ash. Some swirled

into a song-filled pub, inhaled into the red room of a man's
                                                        lungs
and exhaled with a cough before the next verse was begun.

II.

The paper itself was of a cheap batch, thin buttermilk-tint,
bundles bought by Connolly at Swiftbrook Mill.

Every dusk, mill-carts laden with plump sackfuls of rags
would stutter up, ready to be shredded and turned into racks

of paper. From shredded pants and skirts,
from blankets, darned scarves and shirts,

this paper came. From pillowcases, sheets, workmen's
overalls, floor cloths, moth-eaten curtains,

this paper came. From patched fabric, heated
close to the skin of its people,

this paper came. From strips of linen and torn cotton,
this paper came, paper that would hold [dead generations].

In the same year, rags were in great demand
as bandages in the trenches of France

where they were used staunch scalp wounds,
and to soothe eyes from trenches' fumes.

Pyjama pants cut from the same length of linen
may have sent one leg to war and one to the proclamation.

III.

That linen had been pounded, pulled and bleached,
drawn from flax that grew from seed

scattered in a hillside field, seed that grew
into tall stalks and jostled by a wind that blew

eastwards, a wind sharp as the breeze
that would ruffle a dress of red linen years

later, a dress worn by a woman who stood
watching the horizon, with a shawl held at her chin, who

could,

who could almost, almost imagine distant battlefields,
while behind her, flax rippled in a hillside field.

IV.

Into that hillside field, a jagged fragment of paper might fall
from a city starling's singed wing. It might float down to stall

in that seeded dirt – what was once an uttered word,
a rag, a garment, a plant, a seed – finally returned to earth.

FOR OUR SISTERS, ANOTHER PROCLAMATION
(an experimental erasure of the Proclamation of the Irish Republic)

TO   IRELAND,
          IRISHWOMEN:

                   she receives   through us,
          her children   and   her freedom.

                   her secret
          ~~through~~ [threw] her open   and

she now seizes
          her own strength,

     asserted
               in
                    the
                         arms   of
                              every   Irishwoman.
We place
blessing[s]   upon our arms, and we pray
                                   supreme
                         readiness   for the
common good,   worthy of

          A

               LL

AN BONNÁN BUÍ

> *'He would not give me any message except to say,*
> *if I got back to Plunkett in the G.P.O., the words*
> *"Yellow Bittern".'*
> – Bureau of Military History Witness Statement 94,
> Mary McLaughlin.

Our keys to that time are stowed in typed words,
a million one-dimensional syllables printed on the thin sheets
of Proclamations, witness testimonies, pamphlets, records,
but the real stories of our history were stowed in bodies.

Not only in shrapnel scars or smashed glass flinch,
these stories were written deeper within: the long-held breath
still etched in a lung, the involuntary twinge at the smell of
                                                        singed
hair, the muted song that still spins in a cochlea, long supressed.

Still, we attempt to keep written records, to transcribe
the bodies of others to paper, to write their memories
                                                    of events.
One February morning, Ina Connolly-Heron sat by a bedside
and wrote: Miss Mary McLaughlin. Statement.

Mary was feeble, ill, had been bed-ridden for weeks.
Still, she told of her messenger work during the rebellion,
of ammunition delivered to the College of Surgeons, of secret
papers that whispered in her fingers, of Pearse's hand on
                                                    her head when

he said 'God bless you'. She told of hunger and exhaustion,
                                                    of seeing
for the first time in the GPO, a whole salmon laid on a dish.
On sending her with a dispatch for Mc Donagh, she recalled
                                                  a warning
from Plunkett, 'If by any chance you are stopped, eat this,
                                                 swallow it,

but do not let anyone get it'. Her hips remembered the metal heft
of a revolver, found on the cobbles and tucked under her belt.
In her ear, the click of her mother's key, its twist in the lock,
                                          a sound that left
her alone, confined at home, sheltered from battle shells.

Her limbs preserved the sensation of fist-smashed glass, of
                                           leap and sprint
back to Henrietta Lane, through rubble-strewn streets to the
                                                       GPO,
back to Mac Donagh again. She agreed to carry his message
                                               to Plunkett
in her mouth. Who better to keep a secret than a girl of
                                         fifteen? *Yellow*

bittern, yellow bittern, four syllables repeated to herself as she
                                                    tripped
through smoke-streets, past barricades, stumbling over rubble
and crumpled bodies, over torn scraps of the proclamation,
                                         the words gripped
behind her teeth - *yellow bittern.* O yellow bittern, o struggle

of a poet's translated bird who died of thirst, bird who
                                        concealed itself
in reeds, o bird made extinct in famine years, when landlords
drained wetlands, had small fields merged, turned from thin
                                        lengths
into vast pastures to improve yields, o bittern song fading in
                                        discord

as its speckled brothers left, taking with them their lilts and
                                        laments.
Mary ran and ran but never reached the GPO, never passed
                                        those words
from her lips to Plunkett's ear. None of the three ever met
                                        again.
For years, she kept that bird behind her lips, unuttered,
                                        unheard,

neatly folded in the red room of her mouth,
yellow bittern, four lost syllables that grew to live in her body.
When, on a February day, decades later, Ina visits her house
to transcribe Mary's story, she tells it all, finally,

she speaks the secret words that were meant
only for Plunkett's ear. In her mouth, then, the yellow bittern
wakes, shakes its slender speckled wings, trembles, stretches
                                        itself.
Ina leaves, the transcription clipped into a file to be
                                        typewritten.

Returning weeks later for Mary's signature,
Ina is told that she been given an injection of morphine
and can no longer speak. As she leaves, green whispers
shiver in the trees all along the avenue. *Green, green,*

the new leaves quiver. Inside, a yellow bittern clambers
up from Mary's throat and unfurls its spittle-wet wings.
Unseen, it flits under the sash, and swerves
to the lip of the windowsill, where it tilts its head and sings.

AFTER ALL THE PAPERS HAVE BEEN BURNED, WE LOOK WEST TOWARDS INISHBOBUNNAN*

We fall
and go back,
fall and go blank

back through
flame, back
through ash.

If you ask me to tell
you the old name
for that place,

I'll lift
my head

and shake.

---

* *Inishbobunnan, Mayo - Inis Bó Bonnán, Maigh Eo. This placename may be translated as river meadow of cattle and bitterns. Bitterns are now extinct in this area.*

TELLING IT TWICE

The books say that a bittern's song
        can be heard from a distance
of three miles. This bittern's call retells itself
        to me again, repeats, recurs, the same, the same, but
changed. From a hundred years further away,
        I hear it again, doubled, today.

BÉALRÚN

Le linn Aibreán na réabhlóide, líon cúlsráideanna
Bhleá Cliath le tiúin dhifriúil, port na gcos athraithe
go luas níos tapúla, dlús curtha le méadranóm
coiscéimeanna na cathrach. Sciorr scáileanna ó

gach lána mar a rith daoine timpeall ar bharacáidí
ag iompar teachtaireachtaí idir na ceannairí.
D'iompair siad nótaí líonta le horduithe rúnda
folaithe faoina hataí, ina gclupaidí, ina mbróga.

Ritheadar de ráib, a gcuislí ag dordán
ina gcléibh mar phreabadh bodhráin.
Bhí Mary McLaughlin ina measc, cailín
cúig bliana déag d'aois, piostal faoina crios aici.

Faraor, níor éirigh léi an teachtaireacht dheireanach ó bhéal
Mhic Dhonnchadha a chuir i gcluas an Phluincéadaigh.
Ní raibh ann ach ceithre shiolla
– *Yellow Bittern* – teideal dáin a d'aistrigh sé bunaithe

ar an mBonnán Buí. B'iad seo na focail a phioc sé dá chara
agus a gcuid troda ag druidim chun deiridh:
íomhá éin a d'éag de dhíobháil dí,
a chorp spréite ar loch reoite.

Cé gur rith Mary, na siollaí sin á gcogarnaíl aici
faoina fiacail, níor éirigh léi. Gabhadh í ar a slí
ar ais chuig an GPO. Níor chuala an Pluincéadach
riamh an méid a bhí á iompar aici ina béal

dó. Rinne sí béal-rún de agus feadh a saoil,
níor sceith sí an scéal,
cé gur tháinig tocht uirthi gach uair dár chuala sí
cantain na n-éan. Sé seachtainí sular éag sí, scríobh

cara léi cuimhní cinn Mhary. Nuair a d'inis sí an scéal, líon
an t-aer lasmuigh le ceiliúr na n-éan, a ngob ag pléascadh le
caoincí
ceoil. Molaimis na focail fholaithe a choiméad ár sinsir ina
mbéal dúinn.
Molaimis ár gceol, gach siolla agus nóta a ghluais ó ghlúin
go glúin

ó bhéal go béal, a las gach saol le bualadh coiscéime
agus fonn draíochtúil na héanlaithe.
Molaimis na nótaí a chuireann cuisle
fós inár gcroí, agus ceol inár mbéil.

THE SECRETS IN OUR MOUTHS

During that revolutionary April, Dublin's
backstreets filled with a new tune, the daily pace
of steps changed tempo, city feet
became a quickened metronome. Shadows slid

from each laneway, as people darted behind barricades
carrying messages between the leaders, papers
filled with secret orders, hidden under hats,
tucked in pockets, folded below clothes.

They sprinted from shadow to shadow, pulses
thudding like a bodhrán throb behind the breastbone.
Mary McLaughlin was among those messengers,
a girl of fifteen with a pistol tucked under her belt.

She tried, but couldn't deliver the final message
from Mac Donagh's mouth to Plunkett's ear.
It was only four syllables – *Yellow Bittern* –
the title of a poem he had translated

based on the poem *An Bonnán Buí.* These, the last words
chosen by Mac Donagh to send to his friend
as their battle drew to its end: a bird that died of thirst,
its body left stretched on a frozen lake.

Although Mary ran, whispering those four syllables
to herself under her breath, she couldn't deliver the message
before their death. She was captured on her way,
and Plunkett never heard the message in her mouth.

She kept it a secret for all her days. She could never forget
those two words, and each time she heard birdsong,
her breath caught in her chest. Six weeks before she died,
a woman came to write her reminiscences.

On whispering those final words, the air outside brimmed
with birdsong, melodies bursting from beaks, in memory
of those bitterns made extinct. Let us praise the words
that our ancestors kept for us. Let us praise our music,

each syllable and note that moved from mouth to mouth,
from generation to generation, that lit each life with foot-tap
and whistle-lilt. Let us praise the notes that pound under our
                                                        pulse
and tilt song through our mouths and fingertips.

FAILED ELEGY FOR AN ABANDONED LANGUAGE

We cannot lament that which is not

                              dead.

We cannot grieve for that which is still

                    buried in our heads

‑

proclamation unspoken, proclamation of place

[this city lies on ruins] on these streets, we overhear shadows of the old tongue in city talk, a palimpsest [layers of sound in layers of ground – centuries of footfall later, here/hear our feet echo in these same streets] interstices: time lapse, interval, narrow space between parts, chinks of light that glint – where plaster and mortar have fallen away and only thick rocks remain [here, slabs overlap: every cleft, every crevice, culvert and skull, skull and shawl, full and fall, the underneath that sits under these streets under sewage pipes and drains under cellars under concrete paths – the underneath that lurks under cobblestones under layers of mud under dust under dirt], medieval roads where others strode, where others spoke, [where other words filled other throats] in city air other songs sung in older tongue that [brogue erodes] layers – layers [shared between] [before] [soon – beyond] luminous forgotten rooms, [the demolished numinous] we move and move and rearrange, make space for new furniture to sit, to live [this city lies on ruins] [this language lies in ruins]

[CHRONOSEQUENCE]

Here, where decades of diggers' tracks
fill with murky puddles, here,
your phone fails
to find a signal. A starling
flits past. Say *lost*.

> **Strata:**
> This land was
> once an oak forest,
> translated to farmland,
> then swallowed by a profit
> crop of un-baubled
> Christmas trees.
> Say *industrial saws*.

Say *fall* and a scrape scrawls itself
on your hand, red under black mud. The sky darkens.
Follow clawed paw-prints. Think *wolf*. At a crossroads,
choose left. Feel your socks grow wet.
Say *roof* and see it – there – a sudden peak
that tilts the gap between trees. Walk towards it fast,
hoping for a yard with a jeep, a sheepdog, a cup of tea.
Derelict.
The house is an abandoned relic. Uninhabited,
it draws you towards its unlocked door,
as though you could be an owner,
but know that you are a tourist
here, nothing more.   Say *silence*.

Under your fingertips, walls crumble. Say *rubble*
and stumble in. Stair-steps sag underfoot. Say *bed*
and you will see it, still pink-quilted, with a pillow
dotted with fallen plaster. On the sill, a bible lies
open, pages sun-bleached, words evaporated.

Strata:
In layers
of wallpaper,
in repeated splits
of tears from tears,
cleaved from old
paint below,
a broken skin
exposed
to reveal bone-
white plaster
underneath. Feel
this dwelling
shred itself back
to brick, back
to cracked
cement, back
to ground
where,
deep under
wild grass,
roots of oak
are held still
in dirt.

Say *parlour*. There, a chair aims away
from the cracked glass of an ancient TV
and turns towards the window instead.
In wind, a ragged net curtain blows in. Sit.
Sit and imagine yourself become someone
else. Watch the window as they once did.
Birdsong. Nettles and brambles sway. A crab-apple
blossom is drawn through the gap, lifted in
to land in your lap. A gift. Another word
comes to you then, unsummoned: *bláth*.

Strata:
Who could sing,
still, here?
Say *starling*,
bird who fills
air with inherited
sound, speckled
imitations, recalled,
passed down. A bird's
remembered soundscape.
From a stranger's chair,
you listen and translate its song:

sheep's bleat, click of wireless, beer-bottle hiss,
boots clickclack on cobbles, child's giggle,
weep-gulps, stream babble, chicken
-claw scritch-scratch, strike of a match

Say *starling* – starling
who listens, who lifts
shreds of us away,
who records and remembers
sounds we once made. See
this little mimic who will sing
of us to his sons and daughters.
Say *inheritance*.

VOCABULARY LESSONS

do Darach Ó Séaghdha

The Irish for ship is lung.
The Irish for seaweed is famine.
The Irish for hunger has been forgotten.

The Irish for tree is crown.
The Irish for branch is crave.
The Irish for leaves has been erased.

The Irish for silence is _____.
The Irish for wave is tongue.
The Irish for return has become defunct.

The Irish for teach is moon.
The Irish for history is star.
The Irish for reflection is unmarked.

The Irish for secret is ruin.
The Irish for rage is tame.
The Irish for rare is gone – gone,
the mouths, and gone the song.

SPLIT VILLANELLE   WITH TORN TONGUES

Listen. Something [under] our tongues has broken.
We each feel this shared fissure, a fracture, lurking rupture
where something deep within us goes unspoken.

After exams, we throw away textbooks – loathèd, unopened –
and attempt to shed memories of useless vocabularies, cognitive clutter.
Still, something under our tongues is   broken,

sharp, insistent. On these split tongues we are choking.
We swallow all the half-remembered syllables stuttered,   spluttered
and still, something deep within us goes. Unspoken,

now, the hoarded words we learned by heart, the cursèdburden,
all the old stories and strange phrases we once tasted and   turned
like something nearly-sweet under our tongues. It's broken,

the enforced bond that knotted us to that   molten
language. Freed from inherited speech, we shudder,
relieved, but [in this silence] something deep within us goes unspoken.

Despite the relief of freeing ourselves from the curse
of being half-wrong in every borrowed word we utter,
[something] under our tongues [still] persists, [remains]   [unbroken]
something deep within us, whispers itself and exists – spoken.

[A JAW, AJAR]

cur i gcéill: *hypocrisy, bluff*
'Níl i do chuid cainte ach cur i gcéill'
— What you say is a sham

Suppose
you hold a jaw
-bone so old
that the chin has split.

A professor passes samples
of bone around, explains:
derelict workhouse —
Famine-era — a mass grave.

He rattles a transparent plastic bag.
Inside, a clatter of speechless teeth,
a broken grin. He says, *a generous*
selection of fragments, says
incremental dentine collagen analysis.
For him, you must pinpoint when starvation set in.

Suppose you hold the empty jaw bone still,
two neat halves, one in each hand, the pale bone
cool in your palms, three teeth still tucked
into their sockets, snug as heifers
working cud in some distant meadow.

Suppose you hold those jaw bones together
and see it not as a broken, inanimate object
but full, skinned, a stubbled chin, a cheek
that lived, that was patted, kissed, hit,

and between those bones, a mouth
that only ever knew the spit and speech of one
warm, wet tongue. Suppose you hold this split
jaw bone to your ear and imagine you hear
all he spoke, every sound from his throat.

These bones belong to a time
when only Irish was spoken. Holding it, you
want to return to it some of the words that once
resonated through its hollows, but your voice catches
in your throat, as though something inside you
is broken. Suppose the professor approaches,
smiling, as always, says *This is the mandible.*

What would you call that in Gaelic?
You stare at him, bones in hand, your jaw ajar.
Suppose you stutter, your mouth fails. You try
to say *corrán géill,* but the only sound from
your mouth is *cur i gcéill.*

<u>mī-ăz ′mə</u>

mi·as·ma (mī-ăz ′mə, mē-) **n. pl. mi·as·mas** or
mi·as·ma·ta (-mə-tə)

0. Disturbed, this vapour stirs in coil and curve, transparent
swerve & slow uncoil. Shapeless haze, shadowless air. The
Named. The Blamed.

1. A gas of the past, once believed to carry disease (Cholera.
Chlamydia. Black Death.) Rises invisibly from swamps,
from sewers, from supermarket carparks, from puddles on
petrol station forecourts. Process: putrid liquid stirred by
night, stains the air with poisons. Nocturne. This miasma
then moves to infiltrate institutions, to inflict itself upon
the weak, the vulnerable, the usual. Townspeople are
counselled to install windows thick as jam-jars, to smear
glass with clotted honey as a preventative measure against
the encroachment of unsanitary miasmata. In these clear,
sterile, future nights, we select a single antibacterial gel
from dozens on a supermarket shelf. We hurry home and
wipe all surfaces until they gleam, clean of microbes, free
of disease. Miasma: a gas we choose not to see.

2. A cloying vapour that suddenly clutters air, as in a thousand
butterfly wings or bumblebee stings, as in bonfire fog or
geyser steam. This miasma jolts a past physical response
into the present with physical immediacy, engages the
body's memory. Example: the brief delicious inhalation
of a stranger's cigarette smoke by one whose skin still
bears the fossil of nicotine patch stamp. Exposure to such
miasma leaves one lightheaded, with trembling fingers and
quiver-pulse. Pleasure, remembered.

3. A vindictive, harsh atmosphere. The smothering miasma of family, the anxiety that rises from ancestors and is inevitably inhaled by subsequent generations. The inheritance of fear: studies show that when mice are exposed to a stimulus of fear, that in the absence of the original fear trigger, subsequent generations of mice will still display an involuntary startle response following exposure to the same stimuli. Miasma as family fear.

4. Steam of miasma rising from scald-scrubbed hands, in every bubble sheen, shiver-skin, thin tremble of liquid. We cannot clean away our fears. Terrors of disease leak in, invisible as the miasma that infected our ancestors. Though we scoff at their old-fashioned theories of disease, of gaseous contagion, still we respond to their dreads.

5. The instinct that follows a child's child shout, 'Look! I found a bird's leaf. Wet!' and somewhere inside bubbles the memory of a past slapped hand, and screech 'Drop it! Filthy, FILTHY THING.' Instinct brings the same words to a modern mouth. Watch a child run around a garden, feather in fist, trying to fly, restrained by gravity. The fear of that feather, the disease, the extended hand and sweet lure of gratitude to demand compliance: 'TaTa, babba, TaTa'. A parent squirts antibacterial gel, smooths it from one hand to another, four hands in motion, fingers interwoven, foam stroked into each fold, each line. The miasma of anxiety settles unseen into mitochondria, alveolar lacuna, ghosting each synaptic gap.

6. Ever-present anxiety. Fear, inherited.

Doireann Ní Ghríofa

FAOI MHAIGHNÉIDÍN CUISNEORA, TÁ GRIANGHRAF DE MHAMÓ MAR CHAILÍN SCOILE

agus ag cúl an réiteora
tá gríscíní, raca agus rí uaineola
corp agus cnámha, cosa reoite –
bladhm faoi oighear.

Deir céad dlí Newton
go bhfanfaidh gach corp ag gluaiseacht
faoi threoluas mura ngníomhaíonn
fórsa seachtrach air.

Caillte: na crúibíní
a rinne poc-rince ar chliathán cnoic
trí sholas dearg-bhuí
is an ghrian ag dul faoi.

UNDER A FRIDGE MAGNET,
A PHOTO OF GRANDMOTHER AS A
SCHOOLGIRL

and at the back of the freezer
are chops, a rack, and legs of lamb
body and bone, frozen limbs –
a spark in ice.

Newton's first law states
that a body will remain in motion
at the same velocity, unless acted upon
by an external force.

Absent: the hooflets
that skip-jigged over a hill
through the red-yellow light
of sunset.

<u>Deilf</u>

This double-tongue leaves us   cleaved
where twin-words emerge   bound to each
other, Othered –   split between languages –

[a child's drawing: sea
of blue scribbles where a supple muscle
arcs into sky- held there, silver-grey,
astray in air]

                [grandmother's speckled delf,
           dishes that leant against a dresser
      shelf, tangled patterns of the past,
          faint as veins under a wrist]

Where eyes open to dark,   gasp –
a whisper of one word becomes   the breath that lifts
both: a dolphin's lung
soaring   over a sea of splintered
and shattering   blue crockery.

INBOX: 6

'Whatever else is unsure in this stinking dunghill of a world
a mother's love is not.'
– James Joyce, *A Portrait of the Artist as a Young Man*

Subject: two
On 25 Jun 2015, at 23.42
<ashoneill1985@gmail.com> wrote:

It's 11:15 Mam, and as usual there's nothing on except reruns
and repeats. I was just sitting here, flicking from channel to
channel while my work played in a loop from the laptop on
my knee. I lingered on a replay of that documentary where
the old Minister for Finance speaks about the collapse, his
face all yellow with exhaustion and disease. You always liked
him, didn't you? Called him noble, a gentleman. I wanted to
ring you as soon as I saw him, tell you to turn on your telly. He
was talking about going to Brussels as everything fell apart,
about finding himself alone at the airport and looking at the
snow gradually thawing and thinking to myself: this is terrible.
That phrase kept repeating itself to me until I typed it out,
and then I knew I needed to send it to you. An email will
have to do. I couldn't keep watching his pained face so I came
back to this screen, to my last editing assignment, footage of
the aftermath of 1916. It's sort of addictive, seeing all these
familiar streets looking so different, all the gutted buildings
and charred rubble. I pause, zoom in on a barricade, one
of those clots of debris that coagulate like scabs on the old

cobbles. In it, I can make out the edge of a wrought iron bed-head, a hat stand, and a table that might have stood for decades in some maiden aunt's drawing room. Behind the barricade, shadows huddle, guns hoisted.

I'm distracted, as usual, doing three things at once – emailing this to you while glancing between these two screens, from the Minister's face to the shattered black-and-white windows of Liberty Hall. On Sackville Street, a wall falls and a scrawny carthorse staggers under broken wood salvaged from a barricade. Blink- ers, Mam. Blinkers. I watch the wall falling, rewind it until it's intact, then let it fall again. A huddle of long-dead bystanders stand nearby, hands on hips, watching the wall tremble, then crumble at their feet, over and over. My eye remains on the destroyed city, but my mind lingers on that man – broken, ill, alone, waiting to be lifted into the sky.

I think-talk to you all the time but this is the first time I've written to you. I must be really losing it. They say that can happen after a baby, don't they? Depression, delusions... it's all the same, I suppose. Madwoman syndrome. No shortage of that in our gene pool. Haha.

Subject: only me again
On 31 Jun 2015, at 22.12
<ashoneill1985@gmail.com> wrote:

I've ripped through most of what you left me already. I'm flittering away my days in this flat, while your life savings drip away month by month, on rent, supermarket deliveries, bills, takeaways ... I've spent it on running this cocoon suspended high over the city so I can mope and fuck around on the internet and continue to work on a project I'm not even being paid for. Are you ashamed of me? Are you mortified? I'm a mess. I am. I know if you were here you'd say *Everything will be grand*, but I've made such a mess of things this time, I don't even know where to begin. Start at the start they say, so... here's your only daughter, sitting in a dark flat, lit only by the constant loop of the past on a laptop. I still feel like I'm just a daughter, I don't feel grown up enough to be anyone's mother. At your removal, all your friends – Jacinta and Annie, Marian, even Sheila! (I know, she has some cheek to show up after what she did) – they all lined up in the funeral home to grip me by the elbow, hissing that it was *Terrible sad*, that *She'll be missed*, that *She was so proud of you, Ashling*. I knew that, you always told me after a few drinks, all slobbery kisses and hugs and *best daughter ever ever*. You hid it well enough though, always nagging and bitching at me until I escaped the dole queue to scraps of freelance work and this tiny flat. It wasn't much of a jump really and you made sure I never forgot that – no security, no safety net – but I knew you were secretly proud. I knew. Once you left, though, there was no one to make proud anymore. So maybe this mess is actually all your fault for leaving me.

The first time I viewed this flat, it was filled with August sunshine and the river below gleamed blue and free. Chic city living, the estate agent said. Now the river is a slow, murky sludge, hauling itself under the same bridges day after day. Remember how you called my flat *The Tenement* and mimed holding your nose whenever you visited? If I could go back, maybe I'd slap you for all the times you insulted me. You always knew how to wind me up, didn't you? Oh, Mam.

Subject: confessions
On 19 Jul 2015, at 01.42
<ashoneill1985@gmail.com> wrote:

Plural. Five of them. May as well be honest now that you're gone. So, my confessions:

1. I got fired. It was my own fault, I should've kept my mouth shut.

2. I shouldn't be wasting my days tinkering with edits, polishing dissolves between scenes that will never be used. I don't know why I keep working. I miss the job more than I thought I would, and it's not just the small things that I miss – the banter, Friday drinks, the copper jangle of change in my pocket. I miss the person I was in the office. I'm starting to think that's what being grown up is all about, an awful combination of blurting out words you can't take back and then longing for all the lost things you can never get back.

3. I slept with my boss. Once, puking up my hangover in a toilet cubicle, I overheard the part-time receptionist call me brazen. Bitch. She said I only got away with my carry-on because John, the boss, liked my face almost as much as he

liked my arse. What a cow. Still, she was sort of right, I did go off the rails a bit after the funeral ... nothing too serious, just some pills, some wilder nights than usual, but it's true that you wouldn't have been proud of me or my carry-on at work. In fact, you would have probably agreed with that bitch in the bathroom and you could have both torn strips off me together. So yeah, I went a bit crazy for a while, but I still did my work well. On my last project, Women of 1916, footage was so scarce that I had to focus on fading jumpy scraps of old newsreels into photos of female Volunteers, that sort of thing. John said he appreciated my instinct for *timing*, and then, with a slow wink – *when to cut, and when to move on*. He was pretty much as you'd imagine Mam, a bit of a prick, married, paunchy, closer to your age than mine, but still with enough swagger for a quickie every couple of weeks. I don't really know why I liked him, it was something about the way he looked at me, like a bag of chips at 2 a.m. He called an emergency meeting a fortnight after our team had begun working on Women of 1916 and just before he binned the whole idea, he went over the group's work one by one. I'd only done a little bit of the work at that stage but he still praised my edits, especially one shot, dissolving a photo of a woman's face into stock footage of a street scene that showed a stout lady with a big black pram bumping over broken cobbles. He had this way of stroking his chin when he spoke:

'Ah, good old Cathleen Ní Houlihan striding into modern Ireland, with what was probably a pram full of looted spuds, hmmm?'

The others laughed but my smile turned sharp and my hands tightened into fists under the table.

> 'Listen, we need to change our angle. Focusing on the women approach feels ... stale. It's boring. We need to liven it up and focus more on the action, you know? Let's cut what we've done so far and perk things up ...'

Everyone nodded, shrugged, hummed agreement. I don't know why I felt so angry, it wasn't like I wouldn't be paid for my hours on the edits I'd already done.

> 'It's not boring, John, the women's experience of the revolution is so different from what's taught at school.'

> 'Don't be daft, we can get a much more exciting angle.'

> 'Ah John, think of what they gave, carrying the next generation onwards. And think of all they lost, all their partners killed, and all those lost pregnancies from the trauma of the Rising. It's what you always say John, a story that hasn't been told.'

> 'No, no, the doomed romance angle, tearjerker, babies, it's so ... corny.'

He mimed a yawn (told you he was a prick) and turned back to the group.

'Anyway, fine, fine, objection noted from Miss O'Neill. Anyone else?'

I cleared my throat, shook my head. I couldn't let it go. I wish I could go back and slap myself, shut myself up, there had been talk of letting people go for weeks. I can hardly type this without cringing, Mam –

'John. Come on. We can make something of this.'

I felt myself redden as those words left my mouth. When everyone stared at me, I understood that they all knew about us. John just raised an eyebrow, so I stood up and walked out, even slammed the door. I thought he'd come after me, I really did, but I walked home alone, with all the files and footage still on my laptop.

4. Technically, I stole that footage. Not that it mattered really, they had it backed up in the office. The letter came the following day.

As you'll be aware,   recessionary cutbacks
regret
inform you   dissolve our professional relationship.

5. We were never exactly a couple, so I could never have just told him that I was pregnant. I'm not proud of myself, but... it

is what it is. And no, I still haven't told him. Even the thoughts of telling him make me want to throw up. So now here I am, sitting in my flat day and night, my laptop whirring as I stare at these women's faces. I tinker, cut and fade. I imagine the shape the story might have taken.

Subject: an autobiography in selfies
On 21 Jul 2015, at 02.17
<ashoneill1985@gmail.com> wrote:
Attachments: 6 x .jpg

You know what's weird Mam? I spent all day yesterday glancing at my email tab expecting a reply from you, and getting really angry at your silence. You never really got the hang of email though, did you? God, I wish I had your password so I could nose around, read your whole Sent folder. I wonder if anyone else still writes to you... Dunnes Stores loyalty emails, maybe, or porn spam, or unread emails from a secret lover who thinks you're ignoring him. Or is it just me, changing the digit on your inbox from (3) to (4)? It's probably just me. Just me.

Here's all you've missed since you died: – selfie with the Fear – selfie with shots and smeared lipstick – selfie with tayto crumbs – selfie with pee-drenched plastic stick – selfie with laptop working working working – selfie at 4am with screaming infant – selfie as I fall – selfie as I fall apart –

Subject: Tears
On 02 Aug 2015, at 22.10
<ashoneill1985@gmail.com> wrote:

I tore when the baby was born, a second-degree tear from vagina to anus, the doctor said. I was alone, so a midwife held my hand as they sewed the wound, whispering, the stitches will dissolve, it'll all be absorbed into your body, everything will be fine, just fine. It took weeks for my body to mend itself, webbing over the wound to heal me, and the next morning I was still limping as I got ready to leave the hospital. A young nurse lifted the baby from my arms. You have her wrapped all wrong. Here, look. She folded her tiny body in a triangle of blanket, neat as an envelope. I bawled, of course, hot, raw tears. The nurse glanced at the clock. Shush, now. No need to upset yourself. It's just the baby blues. It'll pass, you'll be grand.

Grand. I wish you were still here. It's so much harder since the baby came, I miss you even more and I hate you for not being here to get me to cop on. Since the birth, I dissolve everywhere – in supermarket queues, at the ATM, on buses. I try to stop but it always wins: the rough throat burn, the prickling tear ducts, the itching nose, the trembling lip, the snivelling gasps. Saltwater corrodes me like those old ladders that lead over a pier: rung to rusted rung to crumbling rust down to a vast rolling ocean of nothing. I can't handle the stares my wet face bring, so I just avoid leaving the flat. It's not as strange as it sounds, I can get almost everything I need delivered, and you're footing the bills. The only time I feel like myself is when I'm at home, working instead of thinking.

I know you'd tell me to forget this project, delete it, move on, but I can't. The Women of 1916 file increases every day, a silent growth.

Oh, I named the baby Lily, after Nana. Remember how you used to say that she was in her Mammy's tummy in the Coleraine Street tenements during the fighting of 1916, and that the belly shook so much she always swore that she felt Dublin being torn apart? I think you actually believed that, you were always so bloody gullible. My little Lily is a dote, Mam, you'd be mad about her. She has blue eyes and a little dimple in her chin. I order her these little dresses online, she must be the best-dressed baby in this whole apartment block. Hah! When she dozes, her little fingers grip my thumb like she'll never let me go...

A minute ago, Lily started to stir in her cot, so I fed her and watched this screen darken. Through an opening in the curtains, a sliver of light spilled in. I saw us then, reflected in the empty black screen of the laptop. We looked different, together.

Subject: Attachment
On 01 Sep 2015, at 11.34
<ashoneill1985@gmail.com> wrote:
Attachment: 1916.mov

Last week, Lily learned to laugh. It's a burbly gurgle sort of a sound, like a stream rolling itself into a river. The first time it happened, the sound was so new that it made me jump, but now when she laughs, I can't help but laugh with her. Every day her face grows, it grows more familiar. I've started to see a streak of you in her eyes.

Last night, I turned away from the screens and instead of working, I slept. In my dream, barricades were being dismantled and stacked into bonfires. Since I woke, I've been imagining them on fire, unravelling themselves into wind-sparks. I know what to do now, I'll send the 1916 file to you. I'll attach it to this email and let you take it away from me. Maybe it won't bring anything back, but it'll be a start, Mam. It'll be a start... and maybe then I'll turn off the computer for a while, let it whirr itself into silence.

ACKNOWLEDGEMENTS

My gratitude to the editors of the following literary journals, who featured some of these pieces in their pages: *Banshee, Fallow, Gorse, Mionlach, New Dublin Press, The Stinging Fly, The Trumpet (Poetry Ireland)*.

The poem *Béalrún* was commissioned by TG4 and performed live at the Gradam Ceoil awards for traditional music at the Opera House, and simultaneously broadcast live on television. Buíochas ó chroí le Maggie Breathnach.

The poem *Faoi Mhaighnéidín Cuisneora, Grianghraf de Mhamó mar Chailín Scoile* was selected as the representative poem for Ireland at the Poetry Society's European Literature installation at the British Library in London. My thanks to Judith Palmer. A short film based on the poem can be seen at www.doireannnighriofa.com

Of all the books on 1916 that I read as research for this project, I'd like to acknowledge some sources that I found particularly helpful – *At Home in the Revolution: What Women Said and Did in 1916* by Lucy McDiarmid and *1916 Portraits and Lives* by James Quinn, Larry White and David Rooney (both books published by the RIA). I also enjoyed exploring the first-hand accounts of people who participated in the

Rising at the Bureau of Military History Collection at the Military Archives – a fascinating portal into lives at a time of great change. The Bureau of Military History entry for Mary Mc Loughlin can be read online at:

www.bureauofmilitaryhistory.ie/reels/bmh/BMH.WS0934.
pdf#page=3

Photograph: Marc O'Sullivan

Hugo Hamilton is an Irish novelist and memoir writer. He is best known for his German-Irish memoir *The Speckled People* (2003), which he adapted for the stage and which was first performed at the Gate Theatre in 2012. His latest play *The Mariner* also premiered at the Gate Theatre. His most recent novel *Every Single Minute* (2014) is a fictional account of a journey to Berlin which the author made in 2008 with his fellow Irish writer and memoirist Nuala O'Faolain. He has been awarded numerous international literary prizes, is a member of Aosdána, and lives in Dublin.

Photograph: Tomas Tyner, UCC

Leanne O'Sullivan comes from the Beara Peninsula in West Cork and is the author of three poetry collections, published by Bloodaxe Books – *Waiting for My Clothes* (2004), *Cailleach: The Hag of Beara* (2009) and *The Mining Road* (2013). She has been the recipient of several awards, most recently the Ireland Chair of Poetry Bursary Award (2009, nominated by Michael Longley), The Rooney Prize for Irish Literature (2010), The Lawrence O'Shaughnessy Award for Irish Poetry (2011), and the UCC Alumni Achievement Award (2012).

Photograph: Courtesy of Theo Dorgan

Theo Dorgan is a poet and also a novelist, non-fiction prose writer, editor, translator, broadcaster, librettist and documentary scriptwriter. He has published five books of poetry.

His most recent publications are *Nine Bright Shiners*, (Dedalus Press), the libretto. *Jason and the Argonauts* (Wave Train Press) and *Barefoot Souls*, translations from the French of Maram a-Masri (ARC publications).

His two prose accounts of crossing the Atlantic under sail, *Sailing For Home* and *Time On The Ocean; A Voyage from Cape Horn to Cape Town*, won wide acclaim, as did his recently published first novel, *Making Way* (New Island Books, 2013)

He has been editor of, among other titles, *Foundation Stone: Notes Towards a Constitution for a 21st Century Republic*, *Irish Poetry Since Kavanagh*, *A Book Of Uncommon Prayer*, *What We Found There*, *Watching The River Flow* and, with Gene Lambert, *Leabhar Mór na hÉireann/The Great Book of Ireland*, an unique manuscript volume on vellum.

Awarded the O'Shaughnessy Prize for Poetry in 2010, he was the 2015 winner of the Irish Times Poetry Now Award for the best collection of poetry published in 2014. He is a member of Aosdána.

Doireann Ní Ghríofa is a bilingual writer working both in Irish and English. She frequently participates in cross-disciplinary collaborations, fusing poetry with film, dance, music, and visual art. Awards for her writing include the Rooney Prize for Irish Literature, the Michael Hartnett Poetry Prize, the Ireland Chair of Poetry bursary and a Wigtown Award for Gaelic poetry (Scotland). Her third book *Clasp* was shortlisted for the Irish Times Poetry Award 2016. Her work frequently appears in literary journals internationally, and her poems have been translated into many languages, most recently to French, Macedonian, Gujarati, and English. Doireann's fourth collection *Oighear* is forthcoming from Coiscéim in 2017.